D1320015

Books by Ed Dunlop

The Terrestria Chronicles
The Sword, the Ring, and the Parchment
The Quest for Seven Castles
The Search for Everyman
The Crown of Kuros
The Dragon's Egg
The Golden Lamps
The Great War

Tales from Terrestria
The Quest for Thunder Mountain

Jed Cartwright Adventure Series
The Midnight Escape
The Lost Gold Mine
The Comanche Raiders
The Lighthouse Mystery
The Desperate Slave
The Midnight Rustlers

The Young Refugees Series
Escape to Liechtenstein
The Search for the Silver Eagle
The Incredible Rescues

Sherlock Jones Detective Series
Sherlock Jones and the Assassination Plot
Sherlock Jones and the Willoughby Bank Robbery
Sherlock Jones and the Missing Diamond
Sherlock Jones and the Phantom Airplane
Sherlock Jones and the Hidden Coins
Sherlock Jones and the Odyssey Mystery

The 1,000-Mile Journey

The Great War

THE TERRESTRIA CHRONICLES: BOOK SEVEN

*An allegory
by Ed Dunlop*

cross & crown
PUBLISHING
RINGGOLD, GEORGIA

www.dunlopministries.com
Cover Art by Laura Lea Sencabaugh and Wayne Coley
Poetry on pages 17, 61, and 194 ©Zachary Cox (age 12) Used by permission

The great war : an allegory / by Ed Dunlop.
Dunlop, Ed.
[Ringgold, Ga.] : Cross and Crown Publishing, c2006
215 p. ; 22 cm.
Terrestria chronicles Bk. 7
Dewey Call # 813.54 ISBN 0978552369

When the last battle for Terrestria takes place,
the reader catches just a glimpse of the almighty
power of King Emmanuel and of the wondrous
future that awaits his children
in the Golden City.

Dunlop, Ed.
Middle ages juvenile fiction.
Christian life juvenile fiction.
Allegories.
Fantasy

Expanded Edition
Printed and bound in the United States of America

That my heart

would long for the return

of my King.

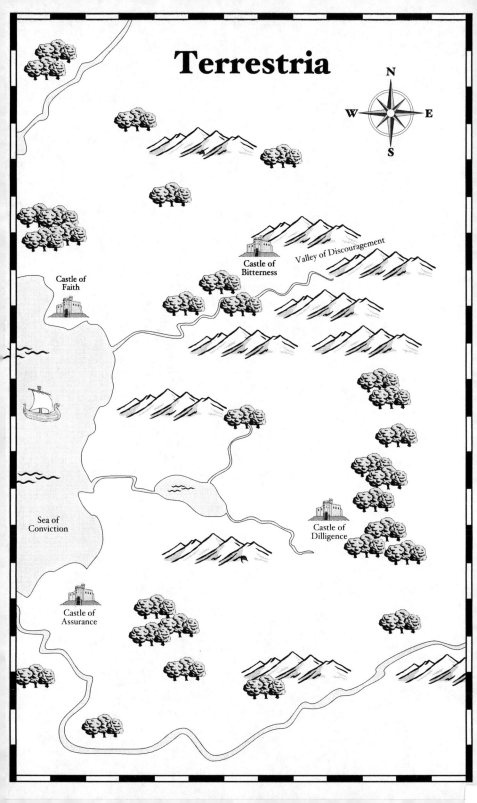

He which testifieth these things

saith, "Surely I come quickly."

Amen. Even so, come, Lord Jesus.

—Revelation 22:20

Chapter One

A fiery streak of brilliant light flashed across the Terrestrian skies as a powerful warrior sped toward the earth like a swooping falcon. Flaring his enormous wings, he banked sharply, slowed, and then hovered briefly as his keen eyes carefully scanned the mountain peak below him. After a moment, satisfied that all was well, he dropped swiftly, silently, to stand upon a jagged outcropping of rock.

Folding his shimmering wings behind him, the figure glanced at the sun as if to check the time of day and then scanned the heavens above him, obviously watching for something or someone.

The tall warrior's finely chiseled features and muscular physique would have drawn attention in any setting, as would his glistening white tunic, had human eyes been capable of seeing him. He drew his glistening sword and slashed the air above his head in a brilliant arc of intense white light and then returned the invincible weapon to its sheath in an action so quick that human eyes would not have seen him move.

He glanced at the sun again, briefly searched the heavens above him, and then dropped to a seat on a large boulder. Turning, he studied the Terrestrian countryside to the west of the mountain.

Far in the distance, a magnificent castle of white stone glistened in the afternoon sun. Situated high atop a rocky palisade that jutted out into a sapphire-blue sea, the castle rose majestically above the surrounding landscape. With its high walls and many towers, the castle was an imposing edifice, visible from many furlongs away. A majestic royal purple standard with the emblem of a cross and crown flew grandly from the top of each tower.

The shining warrior focused his gaze on a lone figure high on the battlements of the castle's northwest tower. As he watched, the person raised his hand toward the heavens. When he opened his hand, an object flashed across the heavens in a thin streak of silver-blue light. The warrior smiled. *Therein lies the strength of this castle*, he told himself. *Oh, that all of Emmanuel's children understood the importance of the petitions!*

At that moment, a second glistening warrior swooped down from the heavens, flared his wings wide, and dropped silently to stand on the rocky ledge before the first warrior. He saluted, and then bowed his head in deference. "Reporting for duty, Captain. I am Olympas."

The Captain turned, and, for several long seconds, looked the second warrior over from head to toe, as if sizing him up. At last, he spoke. "Olympas. From what station of duty do you come, Olympas?" The captain's voice was authoritative and powerful, like the rumble of distant thunder.

Olympas hesitated. "I have not been assigned to active military duty in recent millennia, sire. For the past two thousand years I have been working on new construction in the Golden City of the Redeemed. Housing starts have been down in recent years, sire, and, well, here I am, assigned to a position in your battalion, sire."

"How familiar are you with the present state of affairs in

Terrestria?" the Captain asked.

"I—I have not followed Terrestrian events, sire," Olympas replied a bit nervously. "I—I was told that I would be briefed when I reported for duty."

"And so you shall." The Captain studied the young warrior before him. "How is your swordsmanship? How sharp are your battle skills?"

In reply, Olympas stooped and picked up a handful of pebbles. Hurling them skyward several hundred feet, he paused, and then leaped high into the air. As the pebbles fell past him, his sword slashed the air in lightning-quick movements, neatly slicing each pebble cleanly in two.

Reaching out, the Captain deftly caught several of the remnants as they rained down around him, noting with approval that each had been sliced precisely in half. He nodded as the young warrior dropped lightly to the ground. "Well done. Your sword has not lost its swiftness."

He returned to his seat on the boulder. "Sit down, Olympas. Allow me to bring you up to the present on the state of affairs in Terrestria." He watched as Olympas took a seat on a boulder facing him. "You *are* familiar with the Great War, are you not?"

Olympas nodded. "I am aware of the fact that Terrestria has been at war for centuries, that Argamor still has designs on His Majesty's throne."

The Captain smiled. "The Great War has been raging for centuries, as you said, and yet it is about to culminate in a battle that will involve every man, woman, and child in the kingdom of Terrestria. We stand upon the very threshold of eternity."

"I would appreciate any information you can give me, Captain."

"There are four forces involved in the battle," the Captain said, drawing his sword and sighting along the blade as if to check the edge. "On Emmanuel's side there are the celestial warriors: you and me and the rest of the Host of the Golden City, and also the Terrestrian royalty: those mortals who are Emmanuel's children. Our opposition, of course, consists of the dark warriors: Argamor and all his host of evil, and the peasantry: those Terrestrians who still wear the chains of servitude to Argamor, though some of them may actually think that they have sided with His Majesty."

"Where do I fit in, Captain?" Olympas asked, glancing down at the Terrestrian countryside as if seeing it for the first time. "What is my assignment?"

"You'll be in charge of the garrison of celestial warriors guarding the Castle of Faith," the Captain replied. "You're to replace Tertius, who is being reassigned to the Castle of Assurance. He's to meet with us today in order to help brief you on the affairs of the castle." The huge warrior glanced skyward. "Aye, here comes Tertius now."

As Olympas glanced upward, his face held a look of admiration. "I have heard of this warrior. He is held in high regard."

"With good reason," the other replied. "Tertius is a stalwart warrior, ever alert and watchful, mighty in battle. The dark knights fear his sword as they fear no other. And not only is he a powerful warrior, he is also a brilliant officer—the warriors in the garrison under his command are some of the sharpest in all of Terrestria."

A puzzled look crossed the countenance of the young warrior. "Pray tell, Captain, why is this mighty warrior being relieved of his command at the Castle of Faith?" He frowned. "To tell the whole of it, Captain, I fear that I am unprepared to follow in the footsteps of such a warrior."

The Captain smiled and placed a hand on Olympas' shoulder

to reassure him. "You will do well in this assignment, Olympas. Tertius is being assigned to the Castle of Assurance simply because we are in danger of losing that castle to the enemy. The castle is in jeopardy and requires the might of his sword and the strength of his leadership."

He smiled again. "True, you are lacking in experience, but I think you'll find that Tertius is leaving the Castle of Faith to you in great shape. If you have the leadership skills that we think you have, the garrison of celestial warriors at the Castle of Faith will thrive under your command."

At that moment Tertius dropped from the sky, hovered barely a foot above the mountaintop and saluted smartly, and then stepped down to stand before the Captain. "At your service, Captain."

"As you know, Tertius," the Captain said, without taking the time to acknowledge the salute, "Olympas is to assume your command at the Castle of Faith. I've informed him that the castle defenses are presently quite strong. Am I correct?"

"Aye, Captain," Tertius replied, "that is correct. The garrison is alert and watchful, and the defenses are strong. But only to a certain point, sire."

"Meaning?"

"There is an element of apathy among many of the King's children at the Castle of Faith, as there now seems to be at nearly all the castles. My forces have been seriously limited by their lack of devotion to their King."

A thoughtful look crossed the Captain's face as he considered this bit of information. "Go on."

"The Royal Ones seem to have forgotten that as children of His Majesty they have the right to communicate with their King by sending petitions to the Golden City. Most of them rarely send petitions, and those that do seem to send them out of a sense of duty rather than heartfelt devotion to their King."

He turned to face Olympas. "Behold the Castle of Faith. Do you see the prince upon the battlements of the north wall?"

The three celestial warriors focused their gaze upon the castle. Even though the Castle of Faith was nearly thirty miles away, their incredible vision allowed them to clearly see the lone figure pacing the top of the wall.

"That prince is your main source of power for the defense of the castle. He sends petitions to Emmanuel almost continuously. But for him, I suppose, the Castle of Faith would have already been lost to the enemy."

The Captain leaned forward as he studied the figure upon the wall. "He looks young, Tertius. Who is he?"

"His name is Prince Josiah, sire. He's been a member of the Royal Family for eleven years now, but he has never lost the wonder of his adoption. His heart beats with a fervent love for Emmanuel that few in Terrestria seem to possess today. He lives and breathes to serve his King. Aye, Prince Josiah's petitions are the source of power for this castle. He alone seems to realize the importance of the petitions."

"What are these petitions of which you speak?" Olympas asked Tertius. "I am not familiar with them, yet you speak of them as if they were indispensable."

Tertius stared incredulously at the young warrior for a moment or two and then glanced at the Captain as if to ask for an explanation.

"Olympas has been working construction in the Golden City for the past two millennia," the Captain explained. "As you know, petitions are not used in the Golden City. Explain them to him."

Tertius nodded. "The petitions of which we speak," he told

Olympas, "are a special form of direct communication with His Majesty. They were given to the members of the Royal Family as a special gift and token of his great love for them. Emmanuel has promised his sons and daughters that he will answer their every request and meet their every need, if only they will ask."

The young warrior seemed puzzled. "Are you saying that the Royal Ones do not send these petitions to Emmanuel? Why would they not?"

Tertius shrugged. "You tell me. I have never figured it out."

At that moment, an object shot across the mountaintop in a thin streak of silver-blue light, passing within twenty feet of the three warriors. With a cry of alarm, Olympas instantly dropped to the ground with his sword in his hand. Looking up, he realized that his two companions were still standing, and he slowly got to his feet. "What was that?"

Tertius and the Captain laughed. "That was one of the petitions of which we have been speaking," the Captain replied. "It was sent by the young prince we saw upon the castle wall."

The three warriors took seats upon boulders. Olympas glanced at Tertius and then began to watch the young prince upon the wall of the Castle of Faith. "And you say that this Prince Josiah is the only one who sends petitions?"

"Nay, he's not the only one," the other warrior responded, "but he sends far more than any other resident of the castle. Most of the other castle residents act as if they are too busy to send them."

"It's the same across much of Terrestria," the Captain told Olympas. "Many of Emmanuel's children seem to think that they are too busy to communicate with their King. As a result of their apathy, the kingdom is weakened and Argamor's forces are slowly taking over. Just as he planned, Argamor is conquering Terrestria by stealing the hearts of the people away from their King."

Olympas shook his head. "This is unbelievable."

"Because they lack devotion to their King," the Captain continued, "Emmanuel's children are becoming more and more like the peasants around them. Think of it! King Emmanuel's own sons and daughters, the heirs to the kingdom, living like peasants instead of living as royalty."

"The Royal Ones have forgotten that His Majesty is coming soon to take them to the Golden City of the Redeemed," Tertius commented. "They live as if Terrestria is their home, rather than the Golden City. Rather than setting their affections on things above, as their King commanded them in his book, they have set their affections on things in Terrestria."

The Captain nodded in agreement. "Aye, Tertius, you are right. Indeed, many of the Royal Ones are living for the temporal pleasures and delights of Terrestria, rather than laying up treasure in the Golden City. I agree that perhaps they have forgotten that the Master is coming soon to take them home to the Golden City."

He sighed. "Oh, if only they knew how little time is left! The final battle of the Great War is about to commence, yet the King's children live as if they are totally unaware of what is happening. Their hearts are cold; they have no time to communicate with their King or get to know him by studying his book; they tolerate and even participate in the evil around them. It's no wonder that many of them are losing their children to the enemy." He shook his head sadly.

"But, Captain, some are still loyal to their King," Tertius interrupted. "Prince Josiah is but one of the faithful."

The Captain nodded and smiled. "Aye. The battle is not lost, for His Majesty is returning soon, and the faithful ones will be ready and waiting."

"Do the Royal Ones know about us, Captain?" Olympas inquired.

"They do, but they usually seem unaware of our presence. You must never reveal yourself to them, unless you have direct orders from His Majesty to do so."

"But why, sire? Why should the Royal Ones not see us?"

"Emmanuel has commanded that it be thus."

"I understand that, sire, but why would His Majesty desire that we not reveal ourselves? If the Royal Ones know about us, why should they not see us?"

"Their trust is to be in Emmanuel, not in us," the Captain replied slowly, thoughtfully, "and their praise is to go to Emmanuel, not to us. Perhaps this is why His Majesty has ordered that typically, we are to stay out of sight."

Olympas stood and scanned the countryside. From his vantage, much of Terrestria was visible. "I must ask you a question, Captain. I see before me many, many castles. Is not the kingdom secure with this many castles?"

"You must remember that Argamor is a very subtle adversary," the Captain replied. "Many of the castles that you are now viewing belong to Argamor, although they were built to look like Emmanuel's."

The young warrior frowned. "Argamor's? But—but why does King Emmanuel allow it?"

"Of a truth, I am not sure. But His Majesty knows what he is doing, and we must trust his judgment."

The Captain stood to his feet and flexed his powerful wings. "I must leave for another meeting." Turning to Tertius, he said, "I'll leave it to you to finish briefing Olympas on the castle defenses."

He placed a hand on the younger warrior's shoulder.

"Welcome to Terrestria, Olympas. Tertius will finish briefing you and answer any questions that you might have. Before I go, I must stress one thing—as Tertius has told you, young Prince Josiah's petitions are a source of strength for the Castle of Faith. Make sure that your garrison does everything in your power to protect Josiah. The dark forces will do whatever they can to keep him from petitioning—you and your men must keep them from being successful. Without petitions, the Castle of Faith will be lost."

Prince Josiah descended the castle stairs and turned toward the west bailey. Weary after a long ride from a distant region of Terrestria, the young prince was looking forward to a hot meal and a chance to rest. Having just returned from a mission for Emmanuel, he felt a glow of satisfaction in knowing that he had served his King, but at the same time, he was tired and hungry.

Fifteen paces away, a dark figure waited behind a eucalyptus tree with a sword in his hand. Hidden in the shadows of the tree, he was nearly invisible. As the prince approached, the assailant tensed, ready to spring into action.

Chapter Two

Unaware that he was being watched, Josiah strolled casually across the bailey. In spite of the weariness of his body, his spirit had been refreshed by the brief moments he had spent atop the tower, reading Emmanuel's book and sending petitions to the King. He paused and glanced toward the heavens. Night was falling quickly and numerous twinkling stars were beginning to appear in the darkening skies. To the north he could just make out the constellation that bore King Emmanuel's own coat of arms, the emblem of a cross and a crown. Directly over the castle was Josiah's favorite constellation, the collection of stars that formed the image of a shepherd.

Five paces away, the unseen assailant waited. He raised his sword.

With a deep sigh of contentment, Josiah glanced one last time at the heavens and then started forward, striding directly toward the eucalyptus tree. "Thy children, Lord, are so oppressed," he sang softly. "Oh, come, we plead, and give us rest..."

At that moment the unseen assailant leaped from behind the tree, brandishing his sword and crying, "Surrender, rogue! Surrender your sword at once, or I shall take off your head!"

Josiah stopped and threw his hands into the air to show that he was not resisting. "You have me, my good man," he replied loudly. "I beg for quarter!"

"Surrender your sword at once, or I shall take off your head!" the attacker repeated.

"My sword you shall have, but never in surrender!" Josiah cried, leaping to one side as he reached within his doublet and withdrew his book. In one lightning-quick motion he swung the book, transforming it into a gleaming sword, and then sprang forward to do battle with his assailant. His blade met the blade of the attacker's sword.

"Surrender your sword!" the figure demanded again. "Surrender, sire, or I shall take off your head!"

"Never!" the young prince returned, doing his best to suppress the laughter that threatened to burst forth. "If you desire my sword, you'll have to take it from me by force!"

"Papa, that's not fair!" Josiah's attacker cried, lowering his sword in frustration. "I had you, Papa, and you know it!"

Josiah lowered his own sword, held it against his side to transform it into the book, and then stowed it carefully within his doublet. Laughing, he reached down and swung his diminutive assailant high in the air, ducking his head to evade a blow from the wooden blade that still threatened to do him harm. "Truce, Little Knight!" he called. "Let's call a truce, shall we?"

"Papa, you didn't play fair," the little boy complained, though without a trace of resentment. "I caught you by surprise, Papa. You should have surrendered, but you didn't play fair!"

"You're right, Ethan," Josiah responded, hugging the tyke and then lowering him to the ground to walk beside him. "You did take me by surprise. I had no idea that you were there until you challenged me."

"I challenge you to a duel, sire," the little boy declared, raising his little wooden sword and taking several steps backwards. "If you lose, you must surrender your sword to me!"

"A duel it is, my good man," Josiah replied, reaching within his doublet again. "Prepare to defend yourself, Little Knight, for I'm coming after you!"

Shrieking with laughter, the little boy dashed through the shrubbery, circled around the eucalyptus tree, and ran up behind his father. "I have you, sire," he cried, touching the point of his sword to the small of his father's back. "Surrender your sword, rogue!"

Laughing, the young prince lowered his sword until the point touched the earth. "I surrender," he said with quiet resignation. "You win, Little Knight!"

Lowering his wooden sword, Ethan circled in front of his father and reached for the real sword. "Careful," Josiah cautioned. "It's heavy."

The boy dropped his own sword and grasped his father's sword with both hands in an attempt to raise it. As the blade cleared the ground the little fellow realized just how heavy it was. "Take it, Papa," he implored.

Josiah reached out and took the weapon. "All right, Little Knight," he said with a chuckle.

Ethan retrieved his little wooden sword from the grass. "Papa, when can I be a knight?" he asked. "When can I have a real sword?"

"You'll have to wait a few more years, Little Knight. Right now, why don't we find your mother and then head to the great hall for supper?"

The sound of pleasant laughter came from just beyond the shrubbery, and a slender young woman with long, blond hair stepped into view. A long, flowing gown of pale blue satin and a shawl of exquisite white lace fluttered about her figure. As usual, her cheerful face was graced by a friendly smile of greeting. "Well done, brave knights," she called. "That was quite a duel."

"Gilda!" Josiah exclaimed, taken aback by the sudden appearance of his lovely wife. "Were you watching the entire time?"

She laughed gently. "It was amusing to watch a duel between the two men that I love the most," she replied. She gave Josiah a quick kiss. "You did quite well to go against a knight that is only three years old," she teased. "I was impressed."

Josiah laughed. "Sometimes he seems more like a ten-year-old, doesn't he?" he remarked. "Whatever he does, he does it with all his heart."

"He gets that from his father," she replied earnestly. She glanced at the little boy and then turned back to Josiah. "You know, the other day when the boys of the castle were sword fighting, Ethan was backing down the six-and seven-year-olds! I think they were actually afraid of him."

"He may be little but he wields a fierce sword. Imagine what a knight this little guy is going to be for His Majesty!"

Gilda took her husband's hand. "Come on, supper is ready in the great hall. You're just in time."

"Papa, let's hurry!" Ethan called, running ahead and tugging on the huge door to the great hall. "I'm hungry!"

"We're coming, Little Knight," Josiah replied with a laugh.

At that moment, the door opened to reveal the smiling face of Gilda's brother, Selwyn. "I was just coming to look for you," he told them. "Supper is about to start and it's not like you to be late."

"Uncle Selwyn!" Ethan cried eagerly, leaping up into Selwyn's arms.

Selwyn hugged him. "How are you, Little Knight?"

The little boy leaned away from him with a look of annoyance on his face. "My name is Ethan," he said sternly. "Only Papa calls me 'Little Knight!' That's my special name."

Selwyn laughed. "Aye, your name is Ethan," he agreed. "I'll try to remember to call you that."

"I'll forgive you this time," Ethan replied, throwing his arms around Selwyn's neck for a moment in a fierce hug and then wriggling to be let down.

They entered an immense, open room with a high, expansive ceiling supported by massive beams. At one end of the great hall, a huge hearth blazed brightly with a warm fire. Immense wrought iron chandeliers ablaze with numerous candles hung over the hall from heavy chains. Three rows of long trestle tables flanked by benches occupied the center of the room. King Emmanuel's table, a long table at right angles to the others, enjoyed a place of prominence in front of the huge fireplace. The table was ornate, set with silver service, and flanked by upholstered chairs in place of benches.

Knights and their ladies were strolling casually into the great hall, laughing and conversing warmly with each other. Squires and pages called to each other, and children laughed and chattered happily. Ladies-in-waiting exchanged greetings with members of the castle staff while servants and scullions hurried here and there in preparation for the meal. A minstrel stood in one corner, his fingers flying as he played a cheerful melody on his lute. In the noisy hustle and bustle of the preparation for the evening meal, the atmosphere in the great hall was one of anticipation, happiness, and contentment.

Attendants and pages stood at attention along the walls, and above their heads, the high stone walls of the great hall were adorned with brightly-colored vertical banners of silk and satin. The banners had various emblems embroidered into the fabric, each banner unique and different from its neighbors. Taken from the constellations, each banner was a reminder of King Emmanuel and depicted an aspect of his royal character.

Josiah and his family headed for the King's table. "Ethan," a knight called as the little boy passed his table, "how are you, my little friend?"

"Ethan, my good man, be careful with that sword," another called.

As Selwyn and Ethan walked to their table, numerous people called out to Ethan. It was obvious that the friendly little boy was a favorite at the Castle of Faith. Ethan bowed politely to each of the ladies in turn and shook hands with the men.

"Look at him," Gilda whispered proudly to Josiah. "He acts just like a small knight, doesn't he?"

"Someday he will be a knight, my love," the young prince replied, "so it's never too early for him to behave himself as one."

The prince and his family took their places around the King's table. Lord Watchful, Captain Assurance, Captain Diligence, and their ladies joined them at the table. An attendant rang a silver bell, and the castle's residents quickly took their places around their tables. A hush fell across the great hall.

Sir Faithful, the castle steward, stood to his feet. "We wish to honor our King and show our gratitude for his provision," he announced. The steward held a rolled parchment in his right hand. He opened his hand and the parchment vanished.

Moments later, attendants swarmed around the tables, bearing platters and chargers and large bowls of food. The great hall was filled with tantalizing aromas. Silence soon reigned across the great hall as the castle residents began to enjoy the feast provided by their King.

Ethan eyed the huge chair at the end of the King's table. "Papa, why is King Emmanuel's chair always empty? Where is our King?" The sound of the little boy's voice carried easily across the great hall. Many of the castle residents stopped eating and waited for his father's reply.

"Our King is in the Golden City of the Redeemed, preparing a place for us," Josiah answered, glancing around and realizing that most of the residents were listening to his words. "One day soon, our King will come and take us to the Golden City to live with him."

"Papa, when is the King coming?"

Josiah sighed with longing. "I don't know, Little Knight," he said slowly, "but I wish that he would come tonight. I can hardly wait to see him."

"Papa, I want to see King Emmanuel soon. I love our King."

A hush settled across the great hall as the castle residents pondered the words of the precocious little boy.

The minstrel began to strum softly on his lute. His golden voice filled the great hall as he sang,

"Oh, what a wondrous day that will be
When the face of Emmanuel, my Lord, I shall see.
To stand in his presence, to hear his great voice,
Day of all days, when my heart shall rejoice..."

The meal in the great hall continued in silence as the castle residents ate the delicious feast provided by their King. Josiah stopped eating when the minstrel softly sang another song:

"Thy chosen, Lord, are so oppressed;
Oh come, we plead, and give us rest.
Sinful woes are all around us,
Darkest arts and crimes surround us:
Evil actions, awful motions,

Unclean thoughts and wicked notions;
Sin and sorrow, shame and sadness;
Come, Emmanuel, in gladness!
We long await that blessed day,
When sin and sorrow pass away.
With trumpet sound when we shall rise,
To meet thee there, up in the skies.
When we shall live with thee for ay;
With sin and sorrow passed away.
O haste that day, our sole request
When we shall rise, Thy chosen blest."

Oh, that King Emmanuel would come today, Josiah thought longingly. *I can hardly wait to see him and live in the Golden City with him. Oh, if only he would come back today!*

Chapter Three

Prince Josiah reined his horse, a big bay mare, in close to Selwyn's sleek, black stallion. "Did you just hear a cry for help?"

Both young princes reined their mounts to a standstill. "A cry for help?" Selwyn repeated. "Nay, I heard nothing." He gave Josiah a puzzled look. "Did you hear something?"

"It sounded like a woman's voice," Josiah told him. "I was sure I heard..."

The cry came again.

"Over there!" Selwyn shouted, pointing. "That farm!"

Both men turned their horses and forded a shallow stream that meandered along the side of the road. Riding at full speed they dashed toward a tiny cottage in the center of a small clearing. Dismounting, they ran toward the humble dwelling, and then, hearing a commotion behind the house, ran around the side.

"Leave us alone!" a thin woman screamed at three unkempt-looking men as she attempted to keep them from leading a scraggly brown goat from the farmyard. Seizing the frayed rope tied around the animal's neck, she dug in her heels and pulled against the tall, bearded man who gripped the rope.

"You can't take this goat—she's all we have!" Ten paces away, a small boy stood crying with terror.

Josiah took in the situation at a glance. "Leave this woman alone!" he ordered, striding angrily toward the young ruffians.

Startled, the three rough characters turned at the sound of the young prince's voice. The man holding the lead rope gave a contemptuous laugh. "Well, boys, if it isn't a brace of Emmanuel's men trying to interfere!"

His two companions looked at Selwyn and Josiah with misgiving.

"This doesn't concern you, knaves, so why don't be off about your business?"

"Leave this woman alone," Josiah repeated. "Let the goat go."

"I don't take orders from the likes of you," the ruffian snarled with disdain, "prince or no prince! Now be off about your business."

Josiah stepped toward the man. "I order you to leave this woman alone. Drop the rope."

The ruffian dropped the rope and took two steps away from the goat, then suddenly whirled and leaped toward Josiah with a dagger in his hand. But the young prince was ready and had his sword drawn before the man had taken two steps. The thug skidded to a stop at the sight of the invincible weapon. He swallowed hard, and then quickly regained his composure. "Looks like it's three against two, blokes. Boys…"

His two companions abruptly drew small swords and rushed headlong at the two young princes. Suddenly, the three attackers were clad in dark armor. "For Argamor!" they cried.

Selwyn and Josiah stood shoulder to shoulder as they calmly repelled the attack of the three dark knights. "For the Glory of His Majesty, Emmanuel!" Within moments the attackers realized that they were outmatched and fled through the forest behind the cottage.

Josiah held his sword against his side as it transformed into a book. "Are you all right, my good woman?"

The woman was panting from fear. "I-I'll be all r-right, my l-lord," she stammered, as tears formed in her eyes and then spilled down her cheeks. The little boy dashed across and threw himself against his mother's skirts. Kneeling down, the woman gathered the boy into her arms.

He's just about Ethan's age, Josiah thought.

"How can we thank you, my lords?" Tears streamed down the woman's face. "If you hadn't come just in time, there's no telling what they..."

"We're thankful that we were here to help," Josiah told her. He studied the face of the sobbing little boy. "Is your son all right?"

The mother nodded wordlessly.

"Good woman, if these ruffians should come back, send a petition to His Majesty immediately," the young prince told the distraught mother. "He'll send someone to watch after you and the boy."

"Emmanuel cares about you and your son," Selwyn said.

"I-I should have sent a petition when I saw them coming," the woman replied, wiping tears from her eyes. "As soon as I laid eyes on them I knew they were meant for trouble."

Josiah looked about the little clearing, noting that the garden was well-kept but that the cottage and a tiny lean-to shed were in serious need of repair. "Where is your husband, my good woman?"

"He died last year of a fever," the woman answered slowly. "Now it's just my son and me."

"I'll ask Emmanuel to send a couple of knights to guard you

this evening in case those men come back," Josiah told her. He took a parchment from within his book and quickly wrote a message to the King. Rolling it tightly, he released it to streak across the horizon on its way to the Golden City. "His Majesty will send men to protect you and your farm," he told the trembling mother. "And if you are his child, you have the right to petition him any time you have a need."

The woman nodded tearfully and thanked Josiah and Selwyn again.

A gentle wind was stirring in the treetops as the two young princes rode from the farmyard. "Argamor's men are getting bolder and bolder, aren't they?" Selwyn remarked.

"And lower and lower," Josiah growled in disgust. "Imagine attacking a poor widow woman like that."

Selwyn glanced at the sky. "We have only an hour of daylight left. Let's ride for the Castle of Faith."

The sun was setting as the two princes rode down a gentle slope toward a slow-moving river to rest and water their horses. "Another half an hour and we'll be home," Josiah remarked, looking at the sun. "If we hurry, we might be in time for supper in the great hall. We need to cross the river and head southwest."

"We can ford the river in the shallows there," Selwyn replied, pointing to a crossing a furlong or two downstream. "We'll rest the horses for a moment and allow them to water." Both men put spurs to their horses and rode forward.

As they approached the crossing they heard the sound of angry voices. Josiah slowed his horse to a canter. "There's some sort of commotion," he called to Selwyn. "Let's see what it's all about."

The men rode forward and then reined their horses to a

stop on a steep bank overlooking the river crossing. Wide and shallow at that point, the river was mere inches deep and flowed gently across a gravel bar—the ideal crossing. Three young men were attempting to lead a small flock of sheep through the shallows from the west bank, but another group of sheepherders was keeping them from doing so. A dozen men stood in the center of the crossing, deliberately barring their way. On the east bank waited a larger flock of at least two hundred sheep. The animals were milling about and bleating uncertainly as they waited.

"Use the crossing downstream!" bellowed a stocky sheep-herder in the middle of the stream. "This is our crossing! We've told you this before and we don't intend to tell you again!"

"Our flocks can all cross without trouble," one of the younger men replied imploringly.

"We don't want your mangy animals mixing with ours," the stocky man told him contemptuously. "If both of our flocks cross here, that's exactly what will happen."

"The crossing is wide enough so that our flocks won't mix," the young shepherd replied evenly. "There's no need for trouble. If you want the downstream side of the crossing, we'll take the upstream; if you want the upstream, we'll take the downstream. There'll be no trouble."

"There'll be no trouble because you will not cross here," the man replied. "We aren't taking a chance on mixing our flocks, so just take your filthy sheep down to the next crossing."

"Then we'll wait until you have made the crossing," the youth replied, "but we need to cross here."

"This crossing is ours and you won't use it," the man snarled, "whether we're here or not. We've told you that before. Now, move those wretched animals out of the water and take them downstream as I say."

Josiah rode forward. "What seems to be the trouble?" he called to the youth closest to him.

The young sheepherder splashed through the water as he waded back to the riverbank. "My lord, we go through this every day," he said with a sigh. "These men are from the next village and they insist that this river crossing is theirs and that we have no right to use it. For the last two or three weeks they have been here every time we bring the flock home in the evening, and they always make trouble."

"How far is the next crossing?" Josiah asked.

"More than two miles, my lord. It makes no sense at all to take the flock that far."

Josiah nodded. "That's ridiculous," he agreed.

"My lord, as you can see, this crossing is at least a furlong wide—there's plenty of room for both flocks to cross at the same time with no fear of mixing. Or we could wait until they have finished making the crossing, just as Matthias told them. But they keep insisting that we have no right to use the crossing at all."

"They're just here to make trouble," Selwyn remarked.

The young sheepherder looked up at him. "So it would seem, my lord."

"I'll see what we can do," Josiah said as he rode into the river bottom. He guided his mount around the flock of sheep and rode to the center of the crossing, stopping on a gravel bar that was nearly two hundred yards wide. "What seems to be the trouble, my good man?" he called to the stocky sheepherder who seemed to be the leader.

"There's no trouble, my lord," the man replied with a shrug. "We own this crossing, and we're just asking these lads to use the next one to keep our flocks apart. There's no trouble, my lord."

"Why can't these lads use this crossing?" the young prince

demanded. "This crossing is easily wide enough for both flocks to cross at the same time."

"Our village owns the crossing, my lord. These lads can use the next one."

"Isn't the next crossing more than two miles downstream?" Josiah asked sharply. "You're asking these boys to take their flocks nearly five miles out of the way just to cross the river?"

The man shrugged. "It's our crossing, sire."

"Where are you from, shepherd?"

"We're from the Village of Contention, my lord. It's slightly more than a mile south of here."

"Downstream."

"Aye, my lord."

"So you're asking these lads to take their animals downstream to make a crossing, even though your village is actually closer to that crossing. That's absurd, sir."

The sheepherder shrugged again. "This is our crossing, my lord."

"This river belongs to my father, King Emmanuel," Josiah replied calmly, although inside he was seething with anger at the man's arrogance, "so in reality, the crossing belongs to him." He turned his Shield of Faith so that the man could not miss seeing Emmanuel's coat of arms. "On His Majesty's authority I order you and your men to take your flocks down to the other crossing, which is just as convenient for you and your animals."

"This crossing is ours, my lord."

The young prince let out his breath in an attempt to control his anger. "Do not argue with me, sir. You and your men are to take your flocks to the next crossing. You are not to use this crossing again. If you do, these lads will let me know, and I will deal with you severely."

"The lads can use this crossing, my lord," the man said, throwing his arms wide and smiling disarmingly. "The crossing is plenty wide for all our flocks."

"It is too late for that," Josiah told him sternly. "In your selfishness you tried to hold this crossing for yourselves, just to cause these lads grief. On the authority of His Majesty, King Emmanuel, I tell you that the crossing now belongs to these lads and to this village. You and the people from your village are to use the crossing downstream from this day forward."

The man's face showed his anger. "You can't do this, my lord."

Josiah rode forward. "Take your men and your flocks and move them downstream at once," he ordered.

Selwyn rode his horse into the water and reined in beside Josiah.

Seething with anger, the stocky sheepherder turned and splashed his way furiously across the river crossing. As the young princes watched, the men began to move their flock downstream along the riverbank. When the flock was safely out of the way, Josiah turned to the three young sheepherders. "The crossing is now yours," he told the delighted lads. "Send word to the Castle of Faith if these men ever bother you again."

"You have our gratitude, my lords," one boy called. "We didn't know what to do."

"We were glad to help," Josiah told the boys. "Just let us know if you have any more trouble."

The two young princes made the river crossing and rode up the bank on the eastern side to find a smiling man waiting for them. "My lords, I saw what you did for the lads," he cried, hurrying forward to greet them, "and I am grateful, for actually, you have helped our whole village. These men have caused trouble for many of our people."

"We were glad to help," Josiah replied, reining to a stop beside the man. "But why did you not send a petition to King Emmanuel?"

The villager reacted as if the idea was novel to him. "I guess it just never occurred to us, my lord," he replied.

"His Majesty always stands ready to help," Selwyn told him.

The man nodded. "Aye," he said quietly, "I know he does." Abruptly, he smiled broadly. "My name is Jonah. We are not far from our village and the night is almost upon us—will you do us the honor of lodging tonight in our humble village?"

The two princes looked at each other.

"We're not far from the Castle of Faith, sir," Josiah replied. "I think that we both are anxious to get home tonight. But we are grateful for your hospitality, Jonah."

"Then at least share a meal with us," Jonah implored. "We are humble people, my lord, and the fare will not be elegant, but it will be served with our gratitude. My lords, will you at least allow us this honor?"

Selwyn looked to Josiah to answer.

Josiah nodded. "Of course, sir. We accept your invitation. I am Josiah, son of King Emmanuel, and this is my brother-in-law, Selwyn."

The huge smile returned. "It is a privilege to meet you, my lords. We will be honored to have you in our home."

At that moment the sound of bleating sheep arrested their attention and they all turned to see the small flock of sheep rushing up the riverbank toward them. "We had better move or we'll be trampled by the flock," Jonah told them with a smile as he hurried to one side. "My lords, why don't you follow me to the village?"

Darkness was falling swiftly as the two princes rode slowly

into a peaceful little village following their gregarious guide. Humble daub-and-wattle houses lined both sides of the narrow street. Here and there, cooking fires glowed brightly against the darkness of the coming night and their smoke met overhead to form an undulating gray blanket above the village. Noisy children played in the streets while farmers made their way in from the fields.

"Whoa," Selwyn called gently, guiding his horse around a boy who ran carelessly down the street, rolling a large hoop before him. "Watch where you are going, lad," he called cheerfully to the boy, who turned and gave him a sheepish grin.

"My house is on the next street," Jonah told them. "My wife and my children will be delighted to meet you."

A tall man approached them and Jonah introduced him. "My lords, this is Sisera, our village reeve. Sisera, allow me to introduce two young men who have just come to the aid of our village. Prince Josiah and Prince Selwyn just took care of the trouble that has been brewing at the river crossing." His smile was broad as he went on to tell the reeve about the incident that had just transpired. "So we should have no more trouble from Artemas and the men of the Village of Contention," he finished. "They have been ordered to relinquish the northern crossing to us and use the southern crossing for themselves."

Sisera nodded agreeably. "That is good to hear." He approached the horses and looked up at Selwyn and Josiah. "My lords, we are grateful for your help in this matter. The people of the Village of Contention have caused us no end of grief over the use of that crossing, though it is right beside our village. Again, thank you for your help."

Prince Josiah smiled. "We were glad to be of assistance, sir. And as we told the young sheepherders, if there is any more trouble, simply notify us at the Castle of Faith and we will deal with the matter."

"I am taking the princes to my house to feed them as a small token of our gratitude," Jonah told Sisera. "Surely that is the least we can do."

The reeve nodded and then looked uncomfortable. "My lords, I must ask you to lower your shields as you ride through our humble village."

"Lower our shields? What do you mean, sir?" Josiah was puzzled by the request.

"If you would, my lords, simply ride with your shields face down." The reeve's face and voice betrayed his nervousness. "Just so that Emmanuel's coat of arms is not displayed."

Josiah was incredulous. "Why should His Majesty's coat of arms not be displayed in your village?"

The man stared at the ground, afraid to meet their gaze. "Our local magistrate has decreed that the King's coat of arms shall not be displayed within the walls of our village," he replied in a voice so low that Josiah and Selwyn could barely hear him.

"Your magistrate has decreed this?" Josiah echoed. Anger began to stir within him. "Why should His Majesty's coat of arms not be displayed?"

"There are those within the village who are not loyal to Emmanuel," the reeve replied, holding his hands in front of him as if to make an appeal. "Our magistrate has decreed that Emmanuel's coat of arms must not be publicly displayed in order that these people not be offended."

The two young princes were stunned by the man's words. "His Majesty, King Emmanuel, is Lord of Terrestria, Lord of Eternity," Prince Josiah declared. "How can any magistrate decree that the King's coat of arms be hidden away as if it were an emblem of shame?"

"I'm sorry to tell you this, my lords," the reeve apologized, "but I have my orders. I must ask you to lower your shields."

Josiah was furious. "Sir, please take us to the home of this magistrate at once," he requested. He turned to Jonah. "Forgive us this delay, sir, but this is a matter that we must deal with."

Sisera looked as if he might collapse. "My lords, please. This could stir up a hornet's nest."

Josiah set his jaw. "Then we just might have to kill some hornets."

Chapter Four

Josiah's heart was pounding furiously as he and Selwyn followed the reeve to the home of the village magistrate. "That's where he lives," Sisera told them, pointing to an elaborate home built of stone which stood in sharp contrast to the small daub-and-wattle cottages that lined both sides of the narrow street. "But—" Turning abruptly, he hurried away.

A fat, gaudily dressed man answered the door at their second knock. His fingers were adorned with many rings. "Aye?" he said, hesitantly, looking from Selwyn to Josiah and then back to Jonah. "What is it that you want?" At that point he noticed the regal clothing of the young princes and quickly added, "My lords."

"Thomas, these two men have just done great service to the village," Jonah said hastily, before either prince could say a word. "They have settled the disputes at the river crossing that have troubled our people in recent days and weeks. The men of the Village of Contention will trouble us no more."

"Settled the dispute, have they?" the magistrate repeated. "Indeed." He said the words as if the matter was of no consequence.

"Sir, we have been told that we must not display His Majesty's coat of arms within your village," Josiah said. "We—"

"That is correct," the magistrate interrupted. "No one is to make a public display of Emmanuel's coat of arms in this village."

"Who made this decree?" the young prince demanded. "King Emmanuel is Lord of Terrestria; his coat of arms may be displayed anywhere and at any time."

"Not within this village," the man replied contemptuously.

"Who made this decree?" Josiah demanded again.

"I did," said the magistrate.

"All of Terrestria falls within the realm of His Majesty," Josiah reminded the man. "How dare you presume to make a decree usurping his authority within your little village?"

"There are those within our village who do not even think that this King Emmanuel really exists," the magistrate scoffed. "Why should they be forced to acknowledge his authority when they are not convinced that he is anything more than just a figment of someone's imagination? The very sight of the emblem of the cross and the crown offends these people; therefore, we have decreed that the emblems are not to be publicly displayed."

"You have no authority to make such a decree," Josiah told him sternly. "Your village is under the authority of King Emmanuel, and your people are free to display his coat of arms."

"Your King is not our king," a man's voice said abruptly, and the two young princes spun around to realize that a small crowd was gathering. The speaker, a tall, thin man with graying hair, stepped close to Josiah and shook his fist. "We owe no allegiance to a king who supposedly rules from some imaginary 'Golden City.' I have never seen this Emmanuel, nor have I heard his voice. This ethereal king of yours will not rule my life, nor my village. We will not be ruled by Emmanuel, for Emmanuel does not exist."

"King Emmanuel is Lord of all Terrestria," Josiah replied evenly, "whether or not you choose to recognize his authority in your life. And know this, sir—one day you will bow before His Majesty and confess that he is Lord of Terrestria, even if you have to do it against your will."

"Never!" the man sneered.

Several voices were raised in agreement with the tall man, while most of the villagers who gathered were silent.

"Follow this Emmanuel if you will," another villager told the two young princes, "but don't try to impose his narrow agenda upon us. We will not be ruled by a King whom we have never seen."

"Lower your shields and do not display your King's coat of arms," a woman cried, "for we find this offensive."

"You have a choice as to whether or not you will follow King Emmanuel," Josiah said, raising his voice to be heard by all who had gathered, "but King Emmanuel's followers have a right to speak his name and display his coat of arms."

Selwyn stepped close to Josiah. "Have you noticed that this hostility toward His Majesty is coming from just a few?" he asked quietly. "Most of the villagers are silent. Judging from their reactions, I would say that most are loyal to Emmanuel, or at least compliant, and yet they are afraid to speak out."

Josiah nodded. "It seems that a few villagers who hate the King are imposing their will upon the entire village, and the magistrate is enabling them to do it with this unfair decree."

The crowd suddenly surged forward. "You will not display the coat of arms of Emmanuel in our village!" they cried. "Lower your shields and leave this village at once." Several in the crowd rushed forward as if to do bodily harm to the two visitors.

Josiah drew his sword and Selwyn followed his example. The angry crowd fell back at the sight of the powerful weapons.

"We will leave this village," Josiah declared, "but we will not lower our shields. His Majesty, King Emmanuel, is Lord of Terrestria, and none may destroy the right to proclaim his great name or display his coat of arms."

"I made the decree, and the decree stands," the magistrate replied with a sneer. "No one will display Emmanuel's coat of arms in this village while I am the magistrate."

"His Majesty's coat of arms is being displayed in your village right now," Selwyn told the fat magistrate.

The man's eyes narrowed. "Not in this village," he declared.

"Look at the heavens above you," the prince told him, "for at this moment, the constellation directly over your village is none other than the cross and crown, Emmanuel's own coat of arms. Sir, you cannot eradicate His Majesty's emblems from your village, for to do so, you would have to remove the stars from the sky."

A huge silver moon hung low in the heavens above the Castle of Faith as the two young princes reined their horses to a stop in the center of the drawbridge. "Prince Josiah, is that you?" a sentry called from the gatehouse high overhead.

"Aye," Josiah replied, "and with me is Prince Selwyn."

Chains rattled as the portcullis was raised, and with the creak of hinges, the immense gates parted in the middle to allow them entrance to the castle. Selwyn and Josiah rode into the barbican and dismounted, turning their horses over to the two young stablehands who appeared.

"Josiah, my love, I was worried about you," a gentle voice

said, and Gilda appeared from the shadows.

"Papa!" A small form exploded from the shadows and leaped toward Josiah.

Laughing with delight, the young prince swept the little boy up in his arms and embraced him. "Little Knight, how are you, my good man?"

Ethan coughed directly into his father's face and then tried to cover his mouth. "Pardon me, Papa. I didn't mean to." He coughed again, managing to cover his mouth in time.

Josiah laughed. "It's all right, Little Knight." He looked at Gilda. "That cough doesn't sound too good."

The lovely princess nodded. "He's had it all day. I just hope he isn't catching anything."

"How about a hug for Uncle Selwyn?" Selwyn moved close to Josiah, and Ethan eagerly leaned into his arms, embraced him, and then snuggled up to his father again.

"Papa, where were you? You missed supper in the great hall."

"Aye, Little Knight, I know," Josiah replied. "We tried to hurry, but we ran into some unexpected situations."

"Trouble?" Gilda's eyes reflected her concern. "Did you encounter some of Argamor's men?"

"Aye, there was a bit of a conflict, but not the kind that you would expect. I'll tell you about it shortly."

"I saved some supper for you," she told him, moving close to receive a kiss. She turned to her brother. "Selwyn, you're invited too."

Selwyn grinned. "I thank you, fair maiden. My faint heart and weary body long for refreshment, and the nourishing repast that you have so generously offered will do much to strengthen my feeble limbs and weary—"

"Just come eat, Selwyn," she interrupted him with a laugh.

"It's waiting for you in the great hall."

As the family moved toward the great hall with Josiah carrying his young son, Princess Gilda slipped her hand into her husband's. "So what happened?" she asked. "You're upset about something—I can see it in your eyes."

Prince Josiah sighed to vent his frustration. "Believe it or not, Selwyn and I were told not to display King Emmanuel's coat of arms in one of the villages."

"What?" Gilda stared at him. "What are you talking about?"

Briefly, he told her what had happened.

"That's preposterous!" she exploded, when he had finished. "King Emmanuel is Lord of all Terrestria! How can some pompous magistrate decree that His Majesty's coat of arms is not to be displayed?"

Josiah sighed. "Aye, I know."

Sir Faithful entered the great hall as Josiah and Selwyn were eating. "Ah!" he exclaimed with delight, as he hurried toward their table. "And how was your day, my young friends?" He turned to Ethan, who sat snuggled in his mother's lap. "Where's your sword, Ethan? You always have it with you."

"He's not feeling well," Gilda told the elderly steward. "But as soon as he gets feeling better, I'm sure he'll be ready for a skirmish."

"I'll match swords with you any time you're ready," Sir Faithful told Ethan with a twinkle in his vivid blue eyes. "One day you'll make a stalwart knight for Emmanuel, I'm sure."

He turned to Josiah. "My prince, I need to speak with you when you are finished eating, if I may."

"Sire, I also need to talk with you," Josiah replied. "Can we talk right now?"

The steward nodded and sat down. "Certainly. What's on

your mind? Your thoughts are troubled, I can tell."

"Selwyn and I just came from an incident in a small village that has both of us troubled," the young prince began. Briefly, he told Sir Faithful about the encounter with the men at the river crossing and then of the magistrate's insistence that the King's coat of arms not be displayed within the village. "Sire, what right has this magistrate to decree that His Majesty's coat of arms is not to be publicly displayed? What should we have done, sire? Should we have done battle with the man?"

The steward was thoughtful for several long moments before answering. "First of all, to answer your question, nay, this magistrate has no right to prohibit the public display of Emmanuel's banner or coat of arms. His Majesty is Sovereign Lord of all Terrestria, and that little village certainly falls within his domain. This magistrate was definitely overstepping his authority when he issued his decree." He sighed. "Sadly, this is not an isolated incident. As you know, much of Terrestria is in rebellion against Emmanuel. Other magistrates within the kingdom have made similar misjudgments and issued similar decrees."

"But King Emmanuel made Terrestria, and this kingdom belongs to him," Josiah protested.

"True, and this region of Terrestria was settled and established by royalty, His Majesty's own children," Sir Faithful told him, "not by the peasants who are seeking to banish Emmanuel's influence from the land."

Ethan bent over in a fit of coughing and the old steward looked at him with concern. "That cough sounds rather serious, Gilda."

The princess nodded. "I think I'll take him up to our solar and put him to bed."

Josiah reached for his son, pulled him onto his lap, and

hugged him for a long moment. "Good night, Little Knight," he said gently.

"Papa, will you come up and tuck me in?" Ethan asked, reaching up with both hands and caressing his father's face.

"I'll be up in just a minute, Little Knight," the prince promised. Satisfied, the little boy scrambled down from his father's lap and hurried across the great hall. Reaching the massive front door, he struggled to push it open and then held it for his mother.

Sir Faithful watched with delight. "He's quite the little gentleman, isn't he, Josiah?" he said thoughtfully. "What a knight he will make for Emmanuel's kingdom." Josiah smiled.

"We were talking about the magistrate seeking to ban King Emmanuel's coat of arms from public display," Selwyn remarked, "and you said that peasants in other parts of Terrestria are seeking to do the same. How did we reach this sad state of affairs?"

Sir Faithful sighed. "Apathy. Apathy on the part of royalty, Emmanuel's own sons and daughters, who allowed it to happen by refusing to stand up for what is right. Remember, any time that good men refuse to do what is right, evil will flourish. I'm afraid that's where we find the kingdom today."

He studied the banners on the wall of the great hall for a long moment and then looked again at the two princes. "Do you two remember eavesdropping on Argamor's council of war in Lower Terrestria? Remember the evil plans presented by the Council of Six? Argamor told his warlords at that council of war that he planned to steal the kingdom from Emmanuel by stealing the hearts of Emmanuel's followers. Using the power of the spellavision, the music of the stones, and other evil devices, it seems that he has indeed stolen their hearts. He has destroyed families and weakened the kingdom to the extent that he is now able to attack the castles directly."

The three talked for another moment or two and then Josiah excused himself. "I'll see you tomorrow," he told Selwyn and Sir Faithful. "I have to go up and tuck the Little Knight in."

The late afternoon sun reflected from glittering swords as a dozen young squires practiced their swordsmanship on one another. The hillside just east of the Castle of Faith echoed with the sounds of the conflict. "For King Emmanuel!" the would-be knights called as they faced each other, wielding their swords with such enthusiasm that a spectator would suspect that they really intended to take off each other's heads.

"Let's take a rest, shall we, men?" called Josiah as he took a seat on a huge boulder. "Sit down and catch your breath."

Obediently the boys lowered their swords, held the glittering weapons against their sides as they transformed into books, and then placed them carefully inside their doublets, close to their hearts. The prince did the same with his own sword. Sides heaving as they attempted to catch their breath, the boys found seats in the grass around him.

"Prince Josiah," a servant called, hurrying up the hill to reach him, "your wife has been looking for you. She says that it's urgent."

"Thank you, lad," Josiah told the boy. "All right, men, let's call it a day. Most of you did very well, and you are all showing great improvement. We'll meet again right here on Thursday." After dismissing the squires, he rushed into the castle and dashed up to his solar, taking the stairs two at a time.

As he opened the door, Gilda met him and collapsed in his arms. "Oh, Josiah," she sobbed, "where have you been? We've been looking everywhere for you."

"It's Tuesday," he replied. "I had swordsmanship class on the hillside with the squires. Gilda, what's wrong?"

"It's Ethan," she sobbed. "Josiah, he's getting worse and worse and the physician doesn't know what to do."

Josiah hurried into the room where his son lay curled up on the bed. He took one look and knew that something was desperately wrong. Ethan's face was hot and feverish and his breathing was rapid and shallow. He struggled with each breath. Josiah winced as a racking cough shook the little body.

"Papa's here, Little Knight," he called softly, doing his best to sound cheerful. "How are you feeling?" He sat on the edge of the bed and reached for Ethan.

The little boy scooted close to him. "My throat hurts, Papa," he said in a scratchy whisper, "and I hurt when I breathe. How are you, Papa?"

"I'm fine, Little Knight," Josiah replied, swallowing hard. He could tell that Ethan was sick, seriously sick, and an overwhelming sense of helplessness engulfed him. He took a deep breath. It hurt to see his little boy suffering.

He looked at Gilda. "How long has he been like this?"

"Most of the afternoon, I'm afraid," she answered through her tears. "When I couldn't find you, I sent for the physician, but he's not sure what's wrong with him. Oh, Josiah, what are we going to do?"

Josiah picked Ethan up and cradled the boy's head against his chest. "The only thing I know is to send a petition to Emmanuel," he replied huskily. "He's a very present help in time of trouble."

"You'll get better soon," he promised Ethan, rocking him back and forth. "Papa will send a petition to King Emmanuel and he'll make you better. You'll see." When the little boy didn't answer, Josiah glanced down at him and was surprised to see that he had fallen asleep. Tenderly, he placed his son back in the bed and gently pulled up the coverlet.

"I'm going to the northwest tower to send a petition to His Majesty," he whispered to his wife.

"It's just about time for supper," she replied quietly.

He shook his head. "I won't eat tonight. Do you want me to stay with Ethan while you go eat?"

"I won't eat, either." She fell into his arms. "Oh, Josiah, do you think he's going to be all right?"

"Of course," he reassured her, gently stroking her hair. "I'll send a petition right away. His Majesty has promised to answer, has he not?"

Reassured, she smiled bravely. "Of course, my love. I wish that my faith was as strong as yours."

He hugged her again and then headed for the door. "I'll be up in the tower."

The skies were ablaze with fiery color as Josiah stepped out onto the battlements of the northwest tower. The Castle of Faith lay below him, glowing with brilliant hues of scarlet, gold, and amber from the rays of the setting sun. A gentle breeze stirred, causing the royal purple standard just above his head to ripple gently. Kneeling, he opened his book and withdrew a parchment. Tears filled his eyes as he wrote a desperate message:

"To His Majesty, King Emmanuel,
As you already know, my Lord, my son, Ethan, is very sick.
I tried to be brave for the sake of my wife, but to be honest, I
am very worried. His fever is hot and he struggles to breathe.
The physician does not know what to do. My Lord, would you
please heal my Little Knight? I love him, my Lord, and I thank
you for choosing to send him into our home. Please make him
well again.

Your grateful son, Josiah."

Standing to his feet, the young prince rolled the urgent petition tightly and then released it. A silver streak of light shot across the face of the sunset as the petition sped toward the Golden City. Immediately, Josiah dropped to his knees and began to write another.

Chapter Five

The morning was crisp and cool as the rising sun cast its first golden rays across the towers of the Castle of Faith. Josiah stirred and lifted his head. He opened his eyes, still half asleep, and groggily stared at his surroundings as he tried to figure out where he was. The tower! He was in the northwest tower of the castle. Drowsily, he rose to his feet and rubbed the sleep from his eyes. He frowned in bewilderment. Why would he be in the tower at this time in the morning? Had he spent the night in the tower, and, if so, why?

The petitions! Suddenly, it all came back to him. He had spent the night in the northwest tower of the castle sending petitions to King Emmanuel.

Petitions for what? he wondered. *What would be so important that I would spend the entire night sending petitions?*

Ethan! The petitions were for Ethan! I spent the night sending petitions for Ethan to get well!

Ethan. How was he? "I'm coming, Little Knight," he said aloud as he dashed down the spiral steps. His feet simply would not move fast enough.

Gilda woke as he opened the solar door. Startled, she relaxed as she saw who it was. "Sh-h-h!" She held a finger to her lips.

Josiah's heart was in his throat. "How—how is he?" he asked.

"His fever is down and he's sleeping quietly now," she replied, and her eyes filled with tears as she threw her arms around him. "Oh, Josiah, he's going to be all right!"

"Praise the name of Emmanuel!" the young prince whispered fervently. He held her for a moment longer and then slipped to the side of the bed. "Little Knight," he whispered softly, "you gave us quite a scare." He knelt beside the bed.

Ethan opened his eyes. "Papa!"

"How are you, Little Knight?"

"My throat doesn't hurt any more, Papa. How are you?"

Josiah's eyes filled with tears. "I've never been better, Little Knight," he replied huskily. "I'm doing just fine!"

"Where were you last night, Papa?"

"I sent petitions to the King, asking him to make you better," his father replied. "Emmanuel answered my petitions, didn't he?"

"Aye, Papa." The little boy gazed earnestly at Josiah. "Papa?"

"Aye, Little Knight?"

"Papa, when can I have a sword? A real sword, made of steel?"

Josiah's heart was singing. "I'll tell you what I'm going to do, Little Knight," he said grandly, "I'm going to go talk to Sir Preparation right now and ask him to make you the grandest sword you ever saw. A real sword, just your size!"

The little boy's eyes shone with delight. "Really? A real sword? Made of steel?"

"Made of steel," Josiah replied happily. "You can have it as soon as you get completely well."

"I'm well now, Papa," Ethan said eagerly, as he attempted to get out of bed.

Josiah gently pushed him back. "You had better rest today, Little Knight," he told him. "We'll see how you're feeling tonight."

Josiah hurried down to the armory and described the desired sword to Sir Preparation.

"I'll make it from sheet steel," the crippled little armorer promised, "and I'll hammer it just as thin as I can make it so that it's as light as possible. Then I'll fold it over and braze it closed, so really, it will be a hollow blade." He grinned. "Surely the little fellow can't do much damage with that, can he?"

"That sounds good," Josiah responded. "How soon could you have it ready?"

Sir Preparation shrugged. "How about this evening?"

"Perfect!" Josiah said with delight. "The Little Knight is going to love this!"

Eager for breakfast, Josiah entered the great hall. Selwyn was already there, so Josiah joined him at the table. "How's Ethan?" Selwyn asked.

"He's doing much better," Josiah answered gratefully. "He seems like he's almost his normal self."

Lord Watchful approached their table. "I was going to ask you and Selwyn to ride on a quest for me," he told Josiah, "but I just heard about little Ethan. How is he?"

"He's going to be just fine, sire," Josiah replied. "I petitioned His Majesty last night, and Ethan is much better this morning."

"I'm glad to hear that," the big constable said with relief. "You know, don't you, that everyone in the castle loves that little fellow! We'd sure hate to see anything happen to him."

The young prince smiled. "I thank you, Lord Watchful."

"I'll get someone else to go on this quest with Selwyn."

"No, please don't." Josiah held up one hand. "I'll be glad to go."

"Are you sure?"

"Now that Ethan is getting better, there's no reason I shouldn't go. Besides, it will give me something to do until the sword is ready."

"The sword?"

Josiah told Lord Watchful about the miniature sword that the armorer was making and the man grinned broadly. "Your little fellow will like that."

✦

"So what is this quest on which we now ride?" Selwyn asked, reining the stallion close to Josiah's mare. "All I know is that we're going to the Castle of Diligence, but Lord Watchful didn't tell me any more than that."

"His Majesty wants us to check out the castle's defenses," Josiah replied, "and evaluate their readiness in the event of an attack. I think he also wants us to try to determine if the garrisons of knights need additional training, that sort of thing. Basically, we're just going to do an evaluation of the castle and make sure that they are prepared for an attack by Argamor's forces."

Selwyn frowned. "Is that not the job of their constable?"

"Perhaps he has been lax in fulfilling his duties," Josiah said. "Today that seems to be the situation in many a castle."

The two young princes rode in silence for a few minutes. "It was good to hear that Ethan is doing so much better," Selwyn remarked, as they followed the road over the crest of a hill.

"Praise the name of Emmanuel for that," Josiah replied fervently.

Selwyn stood in the stirrups. "Josiah! Look!"

On the opposite side of the valley stood a castle proudly flying the colors of King Emmanuel. Even from a distance of eight or ten furlongs, both princes could see that the castle was under attack. Hundreds of knights in dark armor surrounded the castle. Three huge catapults and a trebuchet stood facing the castle like giant predator birds preparing to attack. As they watched, two tall siege towers were slowly creeping across the landscape. Scores of dark knights rolled them toward the castle walls. Thud! Thud! Thud! The distant sound of an enormous battering ram striking the castle gates reverberated across the valley.

"The attackers must have caught the castle sentries off guard," Josiah remarked. "They didn't get the drawbridge up in time."

Selwyn drew his sword. "There are only two of us," he said, "but let's ride to the defense of this castle!"

Two powerful warriors with drawn swords sat atop the highest tower of the besieged castle. "So why are we not defending this castle?" one asked. "Is that not what we are here for?"

"The castle residents are not sending petitions," his companion answered with resignation. "We are powerless to act unless they do."

The first shining warrior frowned. "Not sending petitions?"

he echoed. "Do the Royal Ones not realize that they are under attack?"

The taller warrior shrugged. "So it would seem, would it not?" He sighed as he watched the preparations for the battle. "My sword longs to get into the middle of this, but alas, as yet there are no petitions."

Selwyn and Josiah rode across the valley at full gallop. As they drew closer they could see that the battering ram was already making an impact—the castle gates were trembling and splintering under the assault. Scores of archers lined the battlements of the castle, but it seemed that their arrows were having little effect upon the ranks of the dark knights. The enemy arrows were having disastrous effects. Even as the young princes watched, they saw one of Emmanuel's knights after another fall from the castle walls, mortally wounded.

The catapults had been loaded and numerous dark knights worked together to turn huge turnstiles, drawing the long arms of the massive weapons back into firing position. One of the catapults suddenly released and the long arm shot skyward, flinging an enormous boulder over the wall of the castle. The resulting crash from within the castle made Josiah flinch.

"It doesn't look good for the castle!" Selwyn shouted, leaning forward to urge his mount to greater speed.

"May His Majesty help the castle defenders," Josiah replied fervently. "Without his help, the castle doesn't stand a chance." *In my distress I cried unto the King, and he heard me.* The words from the King's book flashed into Josiah's mind almost as if someone had shouted them, and Josiah looked up to see the dove flying overhead. "Send a petition," a still, small voice said, and at that moment, the dove turned and flew into a small tree on a hillock overlooking the battlefield.

Josiah turned his horse. "Selwyn! Follow me!"

The two princes rode swiftly to the top of the little hill and then reined to a halt. "What are we doing?" Selwyn shouted, clutching his sword. "We need to get into the battle! The castle might be lost without us! Let's see if we can take at least one of those catapults out of commission!"

"There's a better way," Prince Josiah declared. "Quickly, Selwyn, get a petition ready!"

Selwyn stared at him. "What?"

"Send a petition," Josiah repeated, snatching his book from within his doublet. Opening the volume, he took out a parchment and wrote a hasty message to the King. He released it and watched as it streaked across the skies.

Following his lead, Selwyn held his sword against his side until it transformed into the book. Within moments, he also had sent an urgent petition. "Keep sending them," Josiah urged. "This is the only possible way that the battle will be won today."

Thoroughly frustrated, the two shining warriors waited impatiently atop the castle tower. "A petition, just send a petition," the taller warrior muttered as he watched the disheartening scene below. "Why, oh why, don't they send petitions?" Glancing across at the towers where a host of other shining warriors waited, he knew that they were just as impatient as he.

Suddenly he leaped to his feet, drawing his enormous sword, which trailed fire and smoke as he raised it. "What is it?" his companion asked, leaping upward into the air and spreading his wings.

"A petition! Someone has sent a petition! This first one is ours—let's go!" Unfurling his mighty wings, he sped like an arrow toward the three deadly catapults. At that moment, the arm of the center catapult shot upright, hurling a huge bolder toward the castle. Banking sharply, the warrior intercepted the deadly missile with his sword raised. With one mighty slash he shattered the boulder into dust, which drifted harmlessly downward.

Wheeling about, he flew like a bolt from a crossbow straight for the spent catapult. The crew of dark knights manning the catapult saw him coming and scattered like chicks before a hawk. With a cry of delight that rang across the battlefield, the celestial warrior swung his sword in a mighty arc, severing the arm of the deadly war machine. He then spun about and hurled his full weight against the catapult. The giant machine toppled over to land on its side with a resounding crash and the sound of splintering wood.

"Take out the catapult to the east," the shining warrior cried to his companion, who had dropped down beside him, "the one to the west is mine!" As the two warriors flew swiftly toward their separate targets, they both saw another pair of warriors swoop down toward the castle entrance.

Reaching the gates, one of the shining warriors seized the end of the huge battering ram and swung it like an enormous club, scattering dark knights left and right. His companion swooped down with drawn sword and flew across the drawbridge. Dark knights tumbled into the moat to escape the power of his sword.

At that moment fully a dozen warriors flew from their lofty perches atop the castle towers and swept through the host of dark knights, dealing death and destruction to the enemy faster than the eye could follow. Within seconds, scores of dark knights lay dead or dying. The remaining host turned and fled for their lives.

The first celestial warrior shot upwards and hovered above the castle. "All hail, Lord Emmanuel!" he cried in a voice that rang like thunder. "The victory is his!" The rest of the shining warriors gathered around him and made the countryside tremble with their shouts of victory and praise.

Prince Josiah had just released a second petition and then cringed as he saw an enormous boulder shoot skyward from the center catapult. His chagrin turned to astonishment as he saw the deadly missile suddenly explode in midair and become a cloud of harmless dust. He glanced toward the center catapult in time to see the arm of the dreaded machine snap in two. An instant later, the giant catapult trembled violently and then toppled over on its side with a loud crash.

"Praise the name of Emmanuel!" he shouted to Selwyn. "Did you see that?"

"Look!" Selwyn shouted, pointing.

Josiah spun around just in time to see the battering ram swing from side to side three times in quick succession, knocking dozens of knights into the castle moat. It then splashed into the moat more than forty yards from the drawbridge as if it had been hurled there by a giant. For some unknown reason, the remaining knights on the drawbridge suddenly tumbled into the moat.

"Look at the catapults and the trebuchet!" Selwyn cried. All four of the dreaded machines of war lay on their sides on the battlefield, broken and useless.

Dark knights by the dozens began to drop. With cries of terror, the rest of the host turned and ran for their lives. Selwyn turned to Josiah. "What—what happened?"

Josiah was speechless for several long seconds. "I—I'm not sure," he stammered, "but I think we just witnessed the power of our petitions!"

⌘

Olympas stood atop the battlements of the Castle of Faith, enjoying the afternoon breezes. A second shining warrior approached respectfully. "I have completed my assessment of the castle defenses, sire," he said eagerly, snapping a crisp salute. "The Castle of Faith is strong, and the celestial warriors are vigilant, though many of the Royal Ones seem complacent and careless."

Olympas nodded.

"Much of the strength of the castle, as you know, sire, is the result of the petitions sent by Prince Josiah."

Olympas nodded again. "The young prince's petitions are the first line of defense."

"Sire," the warrior said suddenly, pointing skyward, "two celestial messengers approach the castle."

Olympas turned, and as he saw the approaching messengers, an intense look crossed his face. The younger warrior noticed. "Sire? What is it, sire?"

"King Emmanuel has sent them to escort one of the castle residents home to the Golden City," Olympas replied quietly. His face took on a thoughtful look. "I wonder who is being summoned by His Majesty."

⌘

Still stunned by the spectacular battle that they had just witnessed, Prince Josiah and Prince Selwyn rode quietly across the drawbridge of the Castle of Faith. When they reached the stables and dismounted, Josiah suddenly remembered the miniature sword for Ethan. "I don't see any stablehands," he told Selwyn. "Would you care for the mare? Sir Preparation should have that new little sword ready for the Little Knight, and I just can't wait to show it to him!"

Selwyn laughed. "Go ahead; I'll take care of it. Next time, it's your turn."

Josiah dashed to the armory. "Sir Preparation?"

The armorer was not there, but a tiny sword lay beside his anvil. Josiah snatched it up. The miniature sword was exquisite, with a gleaming, tapered steel blade and a finely tooled handle of polished brass. Lions and dragons and horses were etched into the hilt alongside King Emmanuel's coat of arms. Three glowing sapphires added to the splendor of the tiny weapon.

Josiah let out his breath in a long sigh of satisfaction. "Thank you, Sir Preparation," he whispered. "Ethan will love this!"

Clutching the tiny sword, he hurried across the east bailey, oblivious to everyone and everything as he anticipated the Little Knight's reaction to the beautiful little sword. Reaching the stairs, he took them two at a time.

Josiah flung open the solar door. "Little Knight," he called, "wait till you see what Papa has for you!"

A wail of anguish stopped him cold like an arrow through the heart. Gilda was down upon the floor of the solar, wailing and rocking back and forth. Dropping the tiny sword behind him, the young prince fell to his knees and threw his arms around Gilda. "Sweetheart!" he cried. "What happened?"

Crying and wailing and rocking back and forth repeatedly, for several long moments Gilda was unable to speak. Josiah waited anxiously. "Gilda, Gilda. What has happened?"

He was not ready for the answer.

"It's Ethan," she sobbed. "He's dead!"

Chapter Six

Josiah struggled to breathe as he and Gilda huddled miserably upon the cold floor of the solar. "Josiah, he's gone," Gilda wailed again. "Ethan is gone!" Her shoulders shook as she sobbed uncontrollably. "What will I do without my son?"

Josiah cleared his throat. "Gilda, the Little Knight is—" A sob choked off his words and he dropped his head, crushing Gilda to himself in a desperate embrace. After several moments, a brilliant splash of color arrested his attention, and he turned his head to see a large, crimson rose lying upon the floor.

He picked it up. "Gilda, look! A rosebud—a perfect rosebud! Where do you suppose it could have come from?"

Sobbing, Gilda took it from his hand. "It's not perfect, Josiah," she said harshly. "Look, it's been crushed on one side. The petals have been bruised." She turned the crimson blossom so that he could see the blemish. "This rose would be perfect, the most beautiful one I've ever seen, but its beauty has been marred."

Josiah extended his hand. "Let me see it, my love."

Josiah's heart leaped as he studied the strange mark on the magnificent rose. "Do you know what this mark is?" he asked, breathlessly. "Gilda, this is His Majesty's coat of arms! Look, it's the cross and crown." He looked at her with an expression of awe written across his features. "This imprint upon the petals could only have been made by King Emmanuel's own signet ring! Gilda, this rose is from the King!"

His wife took the crimson blossom from him. Sobbing, she turned it round and round in her hands.

"Gilda, do you see what this means?" Josiah's voice trembled. "King Emmanuel has taken Ethan to the Golden City, but he left us this rose as a token to comfort us."

Prince Josiah stood like a cold statue as he watched the men of the castle prepare to lower the little bier into the dark hole in the ground. He was beyond tears. Many of his dreams for the future centered in that lifeless little body lying motionless beneath that wretched blue shroud. The Little Knight was gone.

He glanced at the tiny jeweled sword lying across Ethan's chest. *What a knight he was going to be for Emmanuel,* he thought in anguish. *And now he's gone. He never even saw the little sword.*

The tears came quickly, and there was no stopping them.

Gilda took his hand. Selwyn put a hand on his shoulder.

"Wait!" Josiah cried, pulling free from Gilda and Selwyn and dashing across the wooded burial ground.

The pallbearers looked at him in alarm. "My lord?"

"I have to see his face one more time," Josiah sobbed. "I have to see my Little Knight again."

The men hesitated, looked at each other, and then set the bier on the ground. One man knelt and reverently pulled back the shiny blue shroud.

A crushing pressure gripped Josiah's chest as he looked into the peaceful face gently framed by the soft blond hair. "Little Knight," he sobbed. "Oh, my Little Knight!" He reached out a trembling hand and gently touched one shoulder. "Good-bye, Little Knight," he whispered. "I'll see you soon in the Golden City."

"I will come again and receive you unto myself, that where I am, there ye may be also," a gentle voice said, and he looked up into the tear-stained face of Sir Faithful. As he stood to his feet, the old man embraced him. Suddenly, Josiah was at peace.

Moments later, Prince Josiah and Princess Gilda stood weeping at the edge of the moors outside the Castle of Faith as the other castle residents walked tearfully back to the castle. Josiah held his wife close. "Oh, Gilda, I just don't know what we'll do without the Little Knight. I had such plans for him! He was such a happy little boy, so friendly, so energetic... so... filled with life! Everything he did, Sweetheart, he did with all his little heart, and he loved Emmanuel with all his heart! I've never seen another three-year-old like him."

"There never will be another three-year-old like him," she said quietly, and then the tears started again.

Josiah felt a gentle hand on his shoulder and turned to see the bearded face of Sir Faithful. "We—we can't go back to our solar right now," the young prince told the old man. "Would you—would you go to the great hall with us? Just to be alone—you and Gilda and Selwyn and me?"

The gentle steward nodded. "Certainly, Josiah."

The great hall was hushed and empty as the four mourners walked silently to the King's table. Their footsteps echoed across the huge chamber like a hammer on an anvil, and Josiah flinched at the sound.

Josiah and Gilda sat side by side with their arms around each other, consumed by grief and an overwhelming sense of loss. Sir Faithful sat across the table from them and placed his gnarled hands over theirs in an unspoken gesture of concern and caring.

"How did it happen, Gilda?" Josiah whispered. "When Selwyn and I left in the morning, Ethan was getting better. But then when we returned..."

Gilda bit her lip. "His fever came back and then quickly got worse and worse," she sobbed. "I went to the well to get some water for him and when I returned, he..." She stopped for a moment, sobbing, unable to continue. "...he wasn't breathing."

The four sat quietly for several long minutes. The silence in the great hall was almost oppressive.

"Sir Faithful," Josiah asked in a shaking voice, "why did not His Majesty answer my petitions?"

The old man waited patiently, realizing that Josiah had more to say.

"I sent two petitions to Emmanuel on behalf of the Castle of Diligence and he gave an overwhelming victory," the young prince said fiercely. "And yet, when I spent the entire night in the northwest tower sending countless petitions for the life of my son, he didn't answer! Why not?"

Sitting at the end of the table, Selwyn reached out and gripped Josiah's hand. Having witnessed the battle, he knew exactly what Josiah was referring to.

"The Little Knight was the light of our lives, sire! He was so young... so unselfish...so excited about life! He loved King Emmanuel with all his heart and he couldn't wait to become a knight in Emmanuel's service, sire. That's why he wanted the sword so badly..." Josiah fell silent, unable to continue.

"We just don't understand why our King would not answer our petitions for Ethan," Gilda said quietly. "Especially since he answered the two petitions that Josiah sent on behalf of that castle."

"In his great wisdom, His Majesty chose to take little Ethan home to the Golden City," Sir Faithful replied quietly.

Josiah struggled to speak. "Is Ethan—is Ethan in the Golden City with King Emmanuel? We found a rosebud that we believe His Majesty sent us as a token, but...is Ethan really with Emmanuel in the Golden City?"

The old man nodded. "I believe with all my heart that he is."

"How do we know?" Josiah choked on the next words. "Sire, he—he hadn't yet been adopted into the Royal Family. He was not yet a child of Emmanuel."

"You must remember that Ethan was only three years old," Sir Faithful said kindly. "Aye, he was learning to love King Emmanuel, but he still was not quite old enough to choose to be set free and be adopted into the Royal Family. Since he was not yet old enough to make that choice, I believe that His Majesty took him to the Golden City."

"But how do we know that? Does the King's book say that?"

"Nay, not specifically," the steward answered slowly. "But do you remember when King David's young son died? The story is in the first division of your book."

Josiah nodded. "I remember reading that."

"Do you remember what David said when the boy died? 'I shall go to him, but he shall not return to me.' What did David mean by that? He was saying that the little boy would never come back to Terrestria, but that he would one day go to the Golden City to be with the little boy."

Josiah thought it through. "Then one day we will see Ethan again in the Golden City?"

The old man nodded and smiled gently. "That you will, my prince, that you will."

❦

The incoming wave dissolved at Josiah's feet in a surging mass of bubbly white foam. He dug the toe of his boot into the sand and then dragged it backwards, creating a furrow in the sand. The next wave immediately covered the furrow and then dissolved, flowing back out to sea and completely erasing Josiah's work.

"Do you ever feel as if your life is just a mark in the sand?" Gilda asked him. "That nothing you do in life will last beyond the moment in which we now live?"

The young prince frowned. "Why do you say that? What are you thinking?"

"I'm thinking about Ethan. Josiah, he wanted so badly to be a knight and have the chance to serve Emmanuel, and yet, he never got that chance. He'll never grow up and have a family, never have children to carry on his name. Three short years, Josiah, and suddenly he's gone. In just a short while he'll be forgotten."

"He left a lot of fond memories," Josiah replied, "not just for us, but for everyone within the castle. Ethan was loved, Gilda."

"I know," the princess replied bitterly, "so why did Emmanuel take him so suddenly? He never had the opportunity to accomplish anything with his life, to do anything significant, to serve King Emmanuel. It seems horribly unfair for His Majesty to take him so quickly."

Josiah stooped and picked up a brilliant orange starfish, toyed with it for a moment or two, and then flung it out into the waves. "It's hard, Gilda," he said quietly, "but we need to trust our King. He knows what he is doing."

She turned on him in fury. "Maybe you can trust him," she screamed, "but right now, I can't! I just can't! I want my little boy!" Sobbing, she abruptly swayed as if about to fall, but Josiah grabbed her and held her close.

"Sir Faithful said that King Emmanuel took Ethan to the Golden City," she raged, "but why did he? If Emmanuel is the loving King that we have been told that he is, why would he hurt us in this way?"

"Gilda, he didn't do it to hurt us—"

"It's been two days, Josiah," she interrupted him, "two long, horrible days since Ethan was taken from us. I still hurt so badly I can hardly breathe. I've hurt every moment since I found him lying there, so small and so still. Why would Emmanuel do this to us?"

Josiah held her close. "I—I just don't know, Sweetheart."

She pulled away and looked up at him with defiance in her tear-filled eyes. "I can't go on like this, Josiah. Look what our King has done to us! I—I just can't love and serve a King who could be so cruel to his own children. Do what you want, but I've decided that I will no longer serve Emmanuel."

Josiah's heart cried out as he heard the words.

The night was dark. The moon struggled against the clouds that seemed determined to obscure its light, but the clouds were unrelenting. High in the northwest tower, Josiah sighed and scanned the heavens above him, searching for the reassuring presence of the King's constellations. But with the sky so overcast, not a single star was visible.

Hearing the sound of footsteps on the stairs, he turned to see Sir Faithful approaching. "I thought I might find you here, my prince," the steward said quietly. "Josiah, how are you doing?"

Josiah hesitated. "I'm having a hard time with this, sire," he said at last. "Gilda and I both are. We miss Ethan so badly!"

The old man nodded. "I understand. We all miss him, Josiah. He was a splendid little fellow."

"Nay, you don't understand!" Josiah exploded. "It's been more than two days now, sire, and I haven't eaten or slept since he was taken. I hurt so deeply that I don't care if I live or die! Aye, I suppose you miss seeing the Little Knight around the castle, but I miss him so much that I don't think I can live without him!"

"I know that you and Gilda are hurting right now," Sir Faithful said tenderly, "but do remember that Ethan is in the Golden City. He's with Emmanuel."

Josiah clenched his fists. "Sire, let me ask you this—if Emmanuel is the loving King that we think he is, how could he do this to us? This afternoon when we walked the beach, Gilda was asking the very same question. I tried to tell her that we should trust our King, but to be honest, it was just talk for her sake. I'm not sure that I can trust Emmanuel; I'm not sure that I want to serve him any more."

The clouds parted just then, and a brilliant beam of silver light splashed across the battlements of the castle. Sir Faithful glanced upward, and Josiah did likewise. Together they watched as the rift in the clouds grew wider and wider, revealing more and more stars. The effect was that of opening a curtain at an enormous window.

"Look upwards," the old man urged. "What do you see?"

Josiah inhaled sharply. The shepherd constellation, his personal favorite, was perfectly framed in the opening in the clouds.

"What do you see?" Sir Faithful asked again.

"The shepherd constellation."

"And above that?"

Josiah frowned. "Nothing but darkness."

"And because of that darkness," Sir Faithful said softly, "you can see the shepherd." He paused. "Josiah, Emmanuel's plans for you include both dark periods of life as well as light. If all of life were bright and light, there would be no contrasts and life would become tedious. It is only because of the darkness of the night that you can see the shepherd constellation now."

He smiled. "You've never seen the constellations during the daytime, have you?"

Josiah shook his head.

"And why not?"

"The sky is too bright to see them."

"Exactly. Josiah, your King can be trusted. His plans for you may at times include periods of darkness, and periods of pain. Life will bring troubles and sorrows. But during the darkest of times, if you'll look up, you can see the shepherd. Will you trust him?"

Josiah was silent for several minutes. Sir Faithful waited patiently.

"But Emmanuel took Ethan from us," the young prince said at last. "I don't think I *want* to serve him."

"The only other choice is to serve Argamor," the steward replied quietly.

The idea troubled Josiah. "I—I can't do that."

"Oh, Josiah, trust your King," the old man implored. "Remember his great love for you, the love you experienced on the day that he set you free? Remember how easy it was to trust him then? He loves you just as much now, my prince. In this painful trial and in this great loss, he loves you. In the darkness of this night, look up and see the shepherd. Trust him, my prince."

Josiah's eyes filled with tears.

Sir Faithful suddenly leaned forward and peered down into the darkness of the bailey. "Listen, Josiah."

Somewhere in the darkness below, a minstrel was singing. His golden voice and the gentle notes of his lyre wafted across the evening breezes like a melody from the Golden City. The tune was enchanting in its beauty; the words were captivating. Josiah leaned on his elbows and listened as the minstrel sang,

"A fiery bolt of lightning flies
Across the darkened stormy skies!
Sizzling heat and rolling boom
Echo through the rainy gloom.
All the rain is pelting, splashing
While the lightning bolts are flashing..."

That song sounds like my life, Josiah thought mournfully, *and the storm that I'm going through right now.* His heart ached as the song continued.

"Emmanuel's voice in thunder rolls—
Echoing back from hills and knolls!
Leave the thunder to its roaring.
Leave the rain to all its pouring.
Leave the wind to all its slashing.
Leave the lightning to its flashing!
Let the tempest and the gale
Moan and shriek and shout and wail.
Emmanuel is in control
Though lightning flash and thunder roll!
Drop into the sweetest sleep
Emmanuel thy soul will keep."

As the last notes faded away in the darkness, Josiah blinked back tears and looked up at the shepherd constellation. The stars of the constellation seemed so big, so bright, so close... "Emmanuel is in control." The words of the song echoed in his mind, stirring within his soul, comforting and strengthening him.

Sir Faithful moved closer. "Trust in the shepherd, Josiah; rest in his great love for you. In the darkness of this storm, look up and see the shepherd."

"I can't serve Argamor," Josiah said at last. "And if it were not for Emmanuel, I would still be wearing the chain of iniquity and the weight of guilt." He looked upwards at the shepherd constellation. "Give me some time alone, sire. I must send a petition to my King."

Princess Gilda and Prince Josiah walked slowly across the sunny beach. A flock of seagulls circled noisily overhead, screeching and squawking as if they resented the intrusion of the humans. Gilda was quiet. Josiah watched her, trying to determine what she was thinking. "Let's build a castle of sand," he suggested.

She shook her head. "I don't feel like doing that."

He took her hand. "What do you feel like doing?"

"Nothing," she replied. "I really don't feel like doing anything at all." She pulled her hand free, turned, and splashed barefooted into the shallow waves. "Sometimes I wonder if I'll ever feel like doing anything at all, ever again." She turned and looked at him and he saw that her face was hard and cold. "I want my son back."

The young prince sighed. "He's gone, Gilda. As King David

said, 'I shall go to him, but he shall not return to me.' We'll see him again in the Golden City."

"I want to see him now," she shot back. "I don't want to wait years and years until we finally get to the Golden City before I can see Ethan again. I want him now."

He stepped into the water and put his hands on her shoulders. "Sweetheart," he said softly, "Ethan is with Emmanuel. He's happier now than we can imagine. And one day soon, we'll—"

She cut him off. "You talk like you don't even care that he's gone," she said, her voice rising to a shrill pitch. "Josiah, Ethan was our son! He was our only son! He was the sunshine in my day. Each morning when I got up I looked forward to the day just because I would get to spend time with him. Do you know what it was like to get up this morning and realize that he was not there—that I'll never again hear him say 'Good morning, Mama'? You talk like you don't even miss him."

Josiah was weeping inside, but he did his best to keep his emotions in check. "You don't know how much I miss him, Sweetheart," he said in a husky voice. "He was my 'Little Knight.' It was a thrill to my heart just to hear him say the word 'Papa.' I was so proud of him! I'd watch him sword fight with the other little boys in the castle and think, *That little guy is going to make the finest knight that ever served King Emmanuel.* That's gone, Gilda. That dream is gone forever." He choked back a sob. "You don't know how much I miss him."

She turned toward him and started to lift her hand as if to reach out to him, but then she dropped her hand and her face became hard and cold again. "So how can you talk as though everything is just fine? I'm angry, Josiah, angry that Emmanuel would take our little boy when we needed him so. 'Trust Emmanuel, Gilda.' Isn't that what you said yesterday? Well, I can't. I just can't."

Gilda walked out of the water and turned to face him. "I don't think that I want to serve Emmanuel ever again."

She walked away. He started to follow, but she stopped him. "Right now I just want to be left alone."

⁘

Several days later, Josiah and the squires of the castle were engaged in mock battles on the hillside not far from the Castle of Faith. "Take a break, men!" Josiah called to two squires who were battling vigorously. "Gather 'round."

He took a seat on a boulder and the boys obediently took seats in the grass around him. "You're doing well, all of you," he encouraged them. "You'll make fine knights for His Majesty!"

He scanned the group of eager squires. "Marcus, keep your sword a little higher when you go against the enemy."

"Aye, my lord," the boy replied respectfully.

"David, don't hesitate when you start to attack. Move in quickly and put the enemy on the defensive."

"Aye, my lord."

"Nathaniel, I've mentioned this before—stay close to your comrades when you go into a skirmish. If you stay together, their strength is your strength. The enemy will try to divide you, but stay together and fight for each other."

The boy nodded. "Aye, my lord."

Josiah turned and pointed up the hill. "Imagine that the row of little pine trees is the front curtain wall of one of Argamor's castles," he told the squires. "The space in the middle is the main gate. The portcullis is down and the drawbridge is up. The castle is on high alert. You have two hundred men under your command, and His Majesty wants you to storm the castle. Now, what is the first thing you would do?"

The boys sat quietly as they pondered the question.

"I would divide my men into two forces," one boy suggested, "and we would—"

Josiah held up one hand. "What is the *first* thing to do?"

"I would have my men start building a temporary bridge to cross the moat," another boy offered, "and we would—"

"What is the *first* thing to do?"

"I would *start* by placing archers on this side of that ridge," a third boy said, pointing, "and then I—"

"But what is the very first thing you would do *before* you start planning your strategy, or moving your men into position, or... Gentlemen, what is the most important thing you would do before you went into battle?"

The boys looked at him with puzzled expressions.

"The very first thing you would do any time you prepare to go into battle, or any time you are about to be attacked, is to *send a petition* to His Majesty!"

"Aye," several of the boys replied, "we knew that!"

"Then why didn't you say it?" Josiah asked. "I'll tell you why—because you didn't think of it. This is something that every child of Emmanuel knows about, but so often we forget to do it. Gentlemen, as you become knights in His Majesty's service, never forget and never underestimate the importance of sending petitions."

The young prince glanced toward the castle and noticed Selwyn rushing up the hill toward them. The look on his face told Josiah that he was on an errand of great urgency. "Josiah," he panted, as he reached the group, "could I talk with you alone?"

"Sure," Josiah responded. "Boys, that's all for today. Keep practicing your swordsmanship, and never forget the importance of the petitions."

The squires hurried down toward the castle. Josiah turned

to Selwyn. "What's wrong, Selwyn?"

"It's Gilda," Selwyn replied, still out of breath from his dash up the hill. "She left the Castle of Faith!"

"Left the castle?" Josiah failed to see the urgency of Selwyn's message.

"Josiah, she's not coming back!"

Chapter Seven

Prince Josiah stared at his brother-in-law. "What do you mean, Gilda's not coming back?"

"She left this in my solar," Selwyn replied, handing Josiah a parchment. "I found it just moments ago. For some reason, she left it for me to give to you."

Josiah unrolled the parchment. *"My dearest Josiah,"* he read aloud, *"please believe me when I say that I love you, and always will. Your love for me has been a source of strength and blessing, yet I find that I must leave the Castle of Faith, perhaps forever. I cannot stay a moment longer—there are too many memories and too many reminders of our little Ethan."*

Josiah took a deep breath, glanced at Selwyn, and then continued reading. *"I do not know where I shall go or what I shall do. At the moment, my heart is empty and my thoughts are in wild confusion. I know only this—I cannot serve Emmanuel any longer. You and I have both loved and served him, Josiah, and yet, look what he has done to us. How could he take Ethan from us? How could he hurt us in this way?"*

The young prince's eyes filled with tears as he continued to read. *"Please, I beg you, do not try to find me, for that will only bring deeper hurt to both of us. I will always love you, Josiah, but I"* cannot..." Josiah's voice failed him at that point, but he continued to read silently. Tears streamed down his face as he read of Gilda's deep hurt and of the bitterness that she bore in her heart toward her King. When he finished the letter he re-rolled the parchment with trembling hands.

"Josiah, I'm sorry," Selwyn told him, embracing him. "What are we going to do?"

Josiah suddenly felt weary and confused, and overwhelmed by a sense of helplessness. He was encouraged, however, by the fact that Selwyn had used the word *we*. He shook his head and sighed. "I don't know what to do," he replied quietly. "Let's show the letter to Sir Faithful and see what he advises."

The castle steward's face was troubled as he placed Gilda's letter on his desk after reading it. He stroked his beard with one hand while he studied Josiah. "What are you going to do?"

"Sire, I don't know what to do," Josiah replied in anguish. "I want to go after her, to bring her back, to help her love and trust King Emmanuel again, and yet... well, sire, she has asked me not to." Sighing deeply, he held his hands out to Sir Faithful as if to plead for help. "Sire, what can I do? I don't even know where she is, or which direction she is heading."

"The very first thing to do, of course," the old man answered gently, "is to send a petition to Emmanuel. He knows where Gilda is, and he will show us what to do for her."

Josiah nodded. "Of course."

The young prince opened his book and removed a parchment to send a petition to the Golden City. Sir Faithful and Selwyn did likewise. All three knelt and earnestly began to write.

Josiah's eyes again filled with tears as he wrote,

"*King Emmanuel,*

I desperately need your help. Gilda has left the Castle of Faith and I don't know if she is coming back. What am I to do, my Lord? How can I find her, and how can I help her? You know that she loves you, my King, and yet there is such bitterness in her heart because you took Ethan. Keep Gilda safe and bring her safely back to the castle.

What am I to do? Shall I take Selwyn and search for her? Please guide me, lest I make a mistake, and please, watch over my dear Gilda and keep her from harm.

Your son, Josiah."

Rolling the parchment tightly, the young prince released it and watched as it passed right through the castle wall on its way to the Golden City. Immediately, he took a second parchment and began to write another petition.

Princess Gilda and her lady-in-waiting rode along a narrow trail that meandered through a decaying forest. "Shouldn't we start heading back to the castle, my lady?" the lady-in-waiting asked, glancing at the afternoon sky. "We've been gone for almost three hours."

Gilda tossed her head diffidently. "We may never go back to the castle, Miriam."

"Never go back, my lady?" Miriam's face showed her bewilderment. "But the Castle of Faith is your home! Where would we go if we didn't return to the castle? And what would Prince Josiah think if we never returned?"

Suddenly Gilda found herself blinking back tears. "Oh, I don't know, Miriam. I don't know what to think. Losing Ethan has been so hard that sometimes I can't bear it. Part of me wants to return immediately to the Castle of Faith and go on serving

Emmanuel as if nothing had ever happened; and yet, another part of me wants to renounce him forever! Does that make sense?"

Miriam guided her horse around a huge boulder in the middle of the trail. "I don't know, my lady. I'm afraid that I am not prepared to advise you on such matters."

Gilda smiled. "Of course not. I'm just trying to decide what to do, and I suppose I'm just thinking out loud."

"Sometimes it helps just to talk things out, my lady."

"I feel as if King Emmanuel has abandoned me, that he no longer cares what happens to me or how much pain I go through. Why did he take Ethan from me? Josiah and I sent numerous petitions for the life of our son; why did His Majesty not answer our petitions?"

"I'm afraid I have no answers, my lady."

The young princess urged her mount to a canter. "Look," she called, "there's an inn just ahead. Let's stop for a brief rest."

Perched at the side of the road was a small inn half hidden among the trees. With its ivy-covered stone walls and wide, inviting windows, the building had a welcoming, almost friendly appearance. A stately coach stood at the front door with a driver dressed in bright livery waiting patiently nearby.

As the princess and her attendant dismounted in front of the inn, a well-dressed lady exited the building and walked toward the coach. "You look weary, my lady," she said to Gilda as she passed. "Have you been on the road long?"

Gilda nodded. "A few hours. I am a bit saddle sore. We came from the Castle of Faith."

"The Castle of Faith. That is a bit of a trip." The stranger looked her over, noticing her royal garments. "Why does a princess such as yourself travel by horseback, my lady?" she asked with a note of incredulity in her voice. "It's far safer and far more comfortable to travel by coach."

Gilda smiled shyly. "Actually, we hadn't intended to ride this far. I came just to get away from the castle and think through some matters."

The woman stepped close and put a gentle hand on Gilda's arm. "Your countenance tells me that you are troubled, my lady. Is there anything that I might do for you? Sometimes it helps just to have someone to talk to."

Gilda shook her head. "Thank you, but I'll be all right."

"I'm a good listener," the woman persisted.

The princess hesitated. "The telling of the matter might take some time."

"I have no schedule to keep. My time is yours."

An uneasy feeling swept over Gilda like a cold breeze from the north. "I—I don't even know you," she ventured.

"Forgive my rudeness," the stranger replied, fingering a glowing purple pendant that hung from a golden chain around her neck. "In my eagerness to help it seems that I have quite forgotten what is proper. I am Lady Acrimonious, Duchess of Discontent, but to my friends I am Mara. Please, call me Mara."

"Mara," Gilda repeated. "'Tis a pleasant name. My name is Gilda. I am the daughter of King Emmanuel."

"Gilda, my dear," Mara said gently, "will you share your story with me? I can tell that you are going through great difficulties; your pain shows in your eyes. Perhaps I can be of help." She turned to the driver of the coach. "Marcus, Princess Gilda and I are going to have a little chat. Why don't you take her attendant into the inn and ask the innkeeper to provide a bit of refreshment and also care for the horses, and then take the two of us out for a short drive?"

"Aye, my lady."

Mara's coachman ushered Miriam to a table in the dining tavern of the little inn and helped her get comfortable. He then called a servant to attend to her. "You will be cared for superbly," he promised. "The hospitality here is excellent. Please feel free to ask for anything that you require and it will be charged to my mistress. And now, I must attend to the coach."

"It's definitely Gilda and Miriam," Prince Selwyn told Josiah, kneeling in the roadway to study two sets of hoof prints. "The tracks are fresh; I'd say they passed this way within the last three or four hours."

"You're sure?" Josiah queried. He leaned from the saddle and looked again at the tracks.

"Positive," Selwyn replied. "Miriam always rides to the right and slightly behind Gilda, and her mare tends to favor her right rear hoof. It's them, all right."

"Then we're on the right track. That's good to know." Josiah drew his book from within his doublet. "I'm going to send another petition." Moments later, the parchment leaped from his hand.

Selwyn stood upright and hurried toward Josiah. "Open your book again," he said, with a note of excitement in his voice. "Perhaps it will guide us to Gilda!"

Josiah's heart leaped at the idea. He opened the book and eagerly turned it from side to side, watching the volume closely to see which direction caused the pages to glow the brightest. After a moment or two he frowned in bewilderment. "That's strange."

Selwyn stepped closer. "What is it doing?"

"Nothing," Josiah replied. "It's not doing anything at all. No matter which direction I turn it, the pages stay the same." He continued to turn the book from side to side, puzzled by the lack of results.

Selwyn thought it through. "The book was given to us by King Emmanuel to guide our lives," he said slowly, "but perhaps it will not guide us to Gilda."

Josiah glanced at him. "Why wouldn't it?"

Selwyn shrugged, "I don't know. Perhaps it is because Gilda is following the wrong path." He remounted. "Let's continue to try to track her."

Fifteen minutes later, the forest trail crested a small rise. Selwyn, who was in the lead, suddenly reined to a stop. "Josiah, go back," he called urgently. Wheeling his horse around, he rode past Josiah, who turned his own horse and followed Selwyn.

Selwyn dismounted hastily and began to scramble up a nearby tree.

"What in Terrestria?" Josiah called to him, reining to a stop beneath the tree. "Selwyn, what are you doing?"

Selwyn stood on a branch some twenty feet from the ground. Shading his eyes against the afternoon sun, he gazed into the distance. "Josiah," he said in a low voice, "come up here."

Puzzled by his brother-in-law's behavior, Josiah scrambled up the tree after Selwyn. "What is this all about?" he asked, as he reached the branch where Selwyn stood.

Selwyn pointed. "Look."

Josiah turned and looked in the direction Selwyn indicated and then drew in his breath sharply. "Who are they?"

"Argamor's men."

"I know that," Josiah retorted, "but what are they doing here? There must be hundreds of them!"

The wide valley that lay before them extended for several

miles. Pitched in the valley was an enemy camp with row after row of tents. Numerous black pennants and standards flew proudly above the camp, each bearing Argamor's coat of arms, the red dragon. Three enormous catapults and two trebuchets stood in the center of the camp. The huge war machines loomed over the tents like gigantic warriors awaiting marching orders. Even as Josiah and Selwyn watched, two companies of dark warriors marched into the valley.

Josiah's heart pounded. "They're preparing for war!" he declared. "This doesn't look good."

"Perhaps we should head back to the Castle of Faith and alert Sir Watchful," Selwyn suggested. "We're only five miles from the castle."

Josiah thought for a moment and then shook his head. "We can't delay the search for Gilda," he decided. "Let's send a petition to His Majesty."

An alarming thought struck Selwyn and he glanced at Josiah with an anxious look upon his features. "Josiah, they're getting ready to attack the Castle of Faith!"

The young prince swallowed hard. "It looks that way, doesn't it?" He drew a parchment from within his book and hastily wrote a petition to King Emmanuel, telling the King about the enemy forces massing in the valley and then asking again for guidance in finding Gilda. Selwyn joined him in sending a petition of his own.

Moments later the two knelt in the roadway, studying the ground intently as they searched for tracks. "Did they cross the valley?" Josiah asked anxiously.

"I can't tell," Selwyn replied, without looking up. "Their tracks are mingled with other horse tracks at this point." He studied the ground silently for several moments and then laid a hand on Josiah's knee. "We've lost their trail, Josiah. Let's go back to the Castle of Faith and consult with Sir Faithful. We need to tell him about the enemy camp, anyway."

Josiah hesitated. "I hate to abandon the search for Gilda."

"We're not abandoning the search; we're simply going for help."

Josiah grabbed Selwyn's arm in a desperate grip, unintentionally squeezing so hard that his brother-in-law winced in pain. "We have to find her, Selwyn. We have to!"

"We'll find her, Josiah. Come on, let's head back to the Castle of Faith. It will be dark in less than an hour."

The setting sun was painting the skies above the Castle of Faith as the two young princes rode across the drawbridge and entered the castle. Dismounting, they turned their horses over to two servants and then hurried up the stairs to Sir Faithful's solar. "I do hope he's in," Josiah said, knocking upon the castle steward's door.

"Come in, lads, come in," a friendly voice called.

Josiah opened the door and Sir Faithful hurried to meet them. "No sign of Gilda?" he asked, studying their anxious faces.

"Nay, sire. We followed her tracks for awhile, but we lost them less than an hour's ride from here."

The old man embraced him. "I'm sorry, Josiah."

"Sire, we must tell you what we saw," Selwyn blurted, stepping toward Sir Faithful. "Argamor's forces are gathering in a valley just five miles from here! There were hundreds of them, sire, and they have catapults and trebuchets! It's obvious that they're getting ready to attack one of the castles, sire, and we thought that it might very well be the Castle of Faith."

Sir Faithful pondered the information. "How many troops did you see?" he questioned.

"Several hundred, at least," Josiah replied, "but other companies were arriving as we watched."

"It does appear that they are indeed preparing for an assault on a castle," the steward agreed, stroking his beard thoughtfully, "if they have catapults and trebuchets."

"What if they attack the Castle of Faith?" Selwyn asked anxiously.

"Aye, they may. The Castle of Faith is the most strategic castle in this region and they may very well be planning on coming here."

"What are we to do?" Josiah asked.

"At this point we simply send petitions to the Golden City," Sir Faithful replied. "This is His Majesty's war, not ours. We await our orders from him."

"What are we to do to find Gilda?" Josiah asked fearfully. "We must find her, Sir Faithful! We must."

"Gilda is in Emmanuel's hands," Sir Faithful reminded him gently, "and he cares for her far more than you do."

Josiah nodded. "Aye, sire, I know that. And yet, I know that she is in danger, and my heart tells me that I must go to her, but I do not know where to find her. I feel so...so helpless, sire!" He was thoughtful for a long moment. "When we do find her, sire," he said, speaking slowly and anxiously, "what are we to do for her? How can we bring her back to the Castle of Faith?"

Sir Faithful pondered the question. "The decision to return to the Castle of Faith is Gilda's alone," he replied quietly. "You know that you cannot coerce her, or bring her back by force. She must make that decision herself."

The young prince nodded.

"You must encourage her to do what she knows is right," the steward continued. "Deep in her heart, Gilda loves King Emmanuel and wants to please him, but a root of bitterness has sprung up and is troubling her. You may send petitions on her behalf and you may go to her and encourage her, but you cannot force her to do what is right."

"I wrestled with the same feelings of anger toward Emmanuel," Josiah confessed, "but now I am at peace, and I am trusting him again. I know that I shall see Ethan again when I reach the Golden City. Why can Gilda not find that same peace?"

Sir Faithful was thoughtful. "Gilda is a woman," he answered slowly, "and sometimes women struggle more with bitterness than men do. Emmanuel has done her no wrong, but in her heart, Gilda thinks that her King has wronged her, and she finds it hard to accept. For that reason, she is having a hard time trusting her King."

He looked from one young prince to the other. "Bitterness is a terrible weapon in the hands of our adversary, and it seems that he is using it against our dear Gilda. Only the power of His Majesty can set her free."

An abrupt knock at the door startled all three of them. Sir Faithful opened the door to find a young page standing nervously. "The sentry has asked me to alert you, my lord," he told Sir Faithful. "You should know that two horses are approaching the Castle of Faith. One rider is Miriam, Princess Gilda's lady-in-waiting. She is alone, sire. The second horse is riderless."

Chapter Eight

Sir Faithful quickly ushered Miriam into his solar. "Tell us what you know about Gilda's whereabouts," he requested, not bothering to take the time for a proper greeting. "You were with Gilda, but where is she now?"

Gilda's lady-in-waiting looked worried. "I think perhaps Lady Gilda is in serious trouble," the woman replied. "My lady and I had gone for a leisurely ride. She was silent for most of the ride. I could tell that her thoughts were troubled, and I knew that she was thinking of the loss of little Ethan, so I stayed quiet."

Josiah brought the woman a cup of water, which she accepted readily. "I thank you, my lord." After taking a drink, she continued.

"We rode for nearly three hours. She seemed to have no destination, but simply rode anywhere the whim would take her. After a time, we came to an inn, and she determined to stop for a brief rest. As we were preparing to enter the inn, a noblewoman came out, and upon seeing Lady Gilda, engaged her in conversation. My lady went for a ride in this woman's carriage, and that was the last I saw of her."

Miriam looked anxiously from Sir Faithful to Prince Josiah

and then to Prince Selwyn. "I sensed that Lady Gilda was in peril, my lords, and so came as quickly as possible to the Castle of Faith to report the matter."

Sir Faithful nodded. "We are grateful. Miriam, who was this woman?"

"Nay, I do not know, my lord," Miriam replied anxiously. "As far as I know, she was a stranger to us."

"Gilda did not know her?"

Miriam shook her head. "I don't think so, my lord. They greeted each other as strangers would."

"Describe the woman. What did she look like?"

"She was dressed in elegant clothing, my lord, and I took her to be a countess or a duchess. Her coach was also quite elegant. She was tall for a woman, and actually quite handsome, but there was a certain craftiness about her. I can't tell you why, my lord, but there was something about her that suggested that she was deceitful."

"And you're certain that she and Gilda did not know each other?"

"I had never seen her before, my lord, and when she and Lady Gilda met they spoke to each other as strangers." Miriam paused as the incident replayed itself within her memory. "She did introduce herself to Lady Gilda."

Sir Faithful leaned forward. "Did you get her name?"

"Nay, my lord. I was attending to my lady's horse at that moment and didn't hear it."

"You say that Gilda didn't know this woman, and yet she went with her."

"Aye, my lord, she went quite readily. I sensed no hesitation on her part."

Sir Faithful frowned as he considered the information. "Do you have any idea where they were going?"

"Nay, my lord. I did hear the woman tell her driver to take them for a short drive in the coach. When they didn't return shortly, I became concerned."

Sir Faithful was silent for several moments.

Josiah stepped close to Miriam. "Miriam, do you know how to find the inn? Can you take us to it?"

"I—I think so," the woman replied. "We rode on a rather circuitous route going there, but I had no difficulty finding my way back to the castle."

"Let's get some rest," Sir Faithful advised, "and we'll set out for the inn first thing in the morning."

"I want to go now," Josiah replied. "Gilda—" He fell silent.

The castle steward gave him an understanding smile. "There's nothing you can do for Gilda tonight, my prince," he said quietly. "Let's get some rest and start out at first light. The only thing you can do for Gilda tonight is to send petitions to His Majesty."

Mara's coach rolled smoothly down the narrow lane. "This will give us a chance to talk in private," the duchess told Gilda. "My lady, will you tell me your story? What is troubling you so?"

Gilda took a deep breath. "My husband and I live in the Castle of Faith. Three years ago we had a little boy, and we named him Ethan. He was the most darling little fellow that you could ever hope to meet: bright-eyed, friendly, and full of life. He loved everyone he met, and everyone loved him. Whatever he did, he did with all his heart. His one great desire in life was to have a real sword and be a knight in Emmanuel's service." She smiled at the memory. "My husband always called him 'Little Knight,' and the name fit. Mara, he didn't seem like a three-year-old boy, he seemed more like a knight in a small body."

Mara laughed. "He sounds like quite an engaging lad."

Gilda nodded. "As I said, Ethan just didn't seem like a three-year-old. He had a little wooden sword and he loved to engage in mock battles with the other boys of the castle. Mara, he would go against boys that were three and four years older than he, and he would win!"

"I'd love to meet him," Mara said, with a pleasant laugh. "So tell me, my dear, what is troubling you so?"

Gilda sighed. "Ethan is...is gone. King Emmanuel took him from us."

The woman stared at her. "Are you telling me that—"

"Our Little Knight is gone. He's with Emmanuel in the Golden City."

Mara was silent for several long moments. "I'm sorry, my lady. My heart goes out to you. There is no loss as great as the loss of a child."

Tears threatened, but Gilda pushed them back and forced herself to smile. "Mara, I still miss Ethan every moment of every day! They say that time heals all wounds, but I can't imagine getting over the loss of my little boy."

"Not if you loved him as much as you seem to," the woman replied. "Time heals wounds, but only if you are able to forget."

"I can never forget our little Ethan," Gilda vowed.

Mara nodded. "Years from now the hurt will be just as deep as ever. That's only natural."

"Years?" Gilda was aghast. "I don't think that I can bear years of this grief."

"You must remember," Mara said quietly, "that whatever

King Emmanuel does, he does for his own glory."

The young princess nodded. "I know that, and yet—"

"Even when it's not what's best for us," the woman finished.

Gilda stared at her. "Are you saying that His Majesty does not care about us? That possibly he would do something to hurt us?"

"So it would seem, my dear. The loss of your little boy is a wound from which you will never recover, and yet Emmanuel chose to inflict it upon you, did he not?"

Gilda was stunned. "But King Emmanuel has always been so good to us," she argued. "He would never hurt us."

"Emmanuel is good to you when it suits his purposes," Mara said sweetly, "but he can also be cruel when he chooses."

"I am his daughter," Gilda said evenly. "He adopted me, and I am a member of the Royal Family. He knows me and he cares for me. Do you think that he would treat his own daughter with such disregard?"

The other woman smiled at this. "Do you know how many adopted daughters Emmanuel has, scattered here and there across Terrestria? Do you know how many sons he has? They must number in the millions, my dear. Do you really think that he knows and cares for you? He doesn't even know your name."

In spite of the bitterness that she felt toward Emmanuel, Gilda began to grow angry at the words of the woman. "You don't know what you are saying," she retorted, trying to keep her anger in check. "You don't know His Majesty like I do. I am his daughter, and I tell you, King Emmanuel would never hurt us intentionally." A strange emotion stirred within her soul as she said these words.

A haunting smile played upon Mara's lips. "I have known

Emmanuel far longer than you," she said mysteriously, "and I know whereof I speak. Believe me when I say that his plans for you are not always for your own good. He wants you to serve him and he wants to use you like a pawn for his own purposes."

Princess Gilda shook her head. "You are wrong, very wrong," she argued, "for Emmanuel is the most loving King who has ever lived! His thoughts toward us are only thoughts of love and caring, and his plans for us are only for our wellbeing. He—"

Unnoticed by Gilda, Mara fingered the glowing pendant hanging about her neck. Abruptly, an overwhelming sensation of confusion and fear swept over Gilda. Terror seized her, as if she were falling. After a moment, the feeling passed. She turned back to Mara. "What was I saying?"

"You were telling me that Emmanuel loves and cares for you."

"Did I say that?" Gilda responded, as if she could not believe what she was hearing. "Emmanuel does not love me; in fact, I sometimes wonder if he hates me."

"You were saying that Emmanuel would never do anything to hurt you or your husband, and that his plans for you are only for your wellbeing."

"Why would I say that?" Gilda snapped. "There are many times when King Emmanuel has hurt us. In taking Ethan from us he has hurt us terribly. This King of ours can be quite cruel at times, you know."

A look of triumph appeared in the other woman's eyes. "Aye, I know."

A flash of light caught Gilda's attention and she turned just in time to see a white-hot bolt of lightning slash across the darkening skies, followed by a crashing boom of thunder, which seemed to rock the countryside. A gust of wind swept down the side of the canyon, causing the twisted, stunted trees to gyrate and tremble as if stricken with palsy. "A storm is coming," the princess observed. "We had better hurry back to the inn."

"We are close to my castle," Mara replied, looking deeply into Gilda's eyes and fingering the pendant as she said it. "The storms in this region arise without warning, and they can be quite fierce at times. Perhaps you should spend the night at my castle. The innkeeper will see to it that your attendant is looked after."

Gilda hesitated.

"I would consider it an honor to have you as my guest," Mara told her, touching her arm and continuing to stroke the pendant. "Please, do not refuse me this great honor."

The young princess glanced out at the gathering storm. "Perhaps it would be best," she agreed.

Moments later the coach pulled up in front of an imposing edifice. In the subdued light Gilda could see high stone walls and towers nearly obscured by dense tangles of brambles. It was as if the thorny branches had a stranglehold upon the structure and were determined to choke the life out of it. Gilda's heart pounded with fear.

"Perhaps we should..." she began, and then, paralyzed with fear, found that suddenly she could no longer speak. An overwhelming sense of terror consumed her as the coach sped across the drawbridge and entered the castle.

When the vehicle came to a stop within the castle barbican, Mara opened the door and stepped out. "Welcome to the Castle of Bitterness," she said brightly. "'Tis indeed an honor to have a princess such as yourself within its walls."

Gilda alighted from the coach and glanced around uneasily.

The wind howled like a banshee, moaning and groaning in the towers and flinging drops of rain into Gilda's face as if it resented her presence. The skies were dark and the castle seemed to glow with an unearthly gray light. Lightning slashed across the sky and thunder boomed angrily in reply. Fear gnawed at Gilda's heart.

She screamed as her arm was suddenly seized in a strong grip. Turning in terror, she saw that one of the brambles had extended a branch and grabbed her. Desperately she jerked her arm away. A second tendril reached for her, but she leaped clear of the danger. Trembling with terror, she turned to run.

"Hurry along, my lady," Mara urged, tugging at her sleeve. "The storm is almost upon us. If you will follow me, I will show you to your solar in the southeast tower."

Gilda took a deep, sobbing breath and tried to calm her racing heart. Her hostess seemed unperturbed by the attack of the brambles. The princess glanced at the brambles, but they stood motionless. She shook her head. Had she imagined the attack?

As Mara and Gilda hurried up the narrow, spiraling stairs within the tower, a knight brushed past them on his way down. In the gloom of the stairwell Gilda failed to see that his armor was dark and that his coat of arms bore the symbol of the red dragon.

Upon reaching the top of the stairs Mara opened a door and stepped through. Gilda followed her through to find herself in a small, circular room furnished only with a sagging bed and an ancient spinning wheel. "This will be your solar for the night," Mara told her.

Gilda glanced around, noting with misgivings that the tiny room bore a thick coat of dust and that the one narrow window was nearly obscured with spider webs. "It's awfully gloomy," she ventured.

Her hostess laughed. "That's because of the storm," she explained, waving her hand in a casual gesture as if to dismiss the notion. "It will be brighter in the morning. Good night." Without another word she hurried from the room, closing the door behind her. Gilda was dismayed to hear the sound of a key turning in the lock.

"Who is your prisoner?" the knight on the stairs asked as the duchess hurried past him. "Is she royalty?"

"Princess Gilda of the Castle of Faith," Mara replied with delight.

"Never heard of her," the knight replied.

"She is the wife of Prince Josiah of the Castle of Faith," Mara informed him.

The man's eyes widened. "The petitioning prince?"

"None other!" Mara's smile was one of triumph.

The knight frowned. "The princess is of no consequence," he stated flatly. "Would we not have done better to capture her husband?"

"Simpleton," Mara hissed, stepping close to the knight. "When we destroy the princess, we defeat her husband. When Prince Josiah ceases sending petitions, the Castle of Faith will fall into Lord Argamor's hands. And when the castle falls, it will only be a matter of time before Lord Argamor will control the entire kingdom of Terrestria."

Chapter Nine

"The innkeeper said that the castle was just beyond this valley," Josiah said to Selwyn, hurrying to catch up with him. "But how do we know that this is the right castle? And what if Gilda did not go with this Lady Acrimonious person?"

"The carriage tracks lead from the inn right to this point," Selwyn replied, glancing at the ground to determine that he was still following the trail. "The innkeeper and Miriam both said that Gilda went with her, though Miriam did not know her name. Quit worrying, Josiah—we'll find her."

"If the countess has harmed Gilda—" Josiah didn't finish the sentence.

"Gilda may be the prisoner of Lady Acrimonious, but she's in Emmanuel's hands," Selwyn reminded him. "His Majesty can protect Gilda. Trust him."

Josiah smiled. "I know, Selwyn, but sometimes it's easier to say than to do. And you heard what the innkeeper said: many times when the countess takes a prisoner, that person is never seen again."

The path wound its way down through a narrow, wooded glen bounded on both sides by steep slopes covered with thorn trees and brambles. The ground was soggy, oozing brackish water at every step that Josiah and Selwyn took. The air became cold and the young princes gathered their cloaks more tightly about them. To the east the sky was bright and sunny, but darkness hovered over the glen, causing Josiah's feelings of trepidation to increase. He shivered and pressed forward, determined not to fail in his quest to rescue Gilda.

The brambles grew denser, in some places nearly blocking the trail. Before long, Josiah and Selwyn were struggling just to make headway. The sharp thorns tore at their faces and clothing, clutching at them as if determined to keep them from passing that way. Soon their hands and arms were torn and bleeding. The brambles were now so thick that the path was virtually impassable, and the carriage tracks were no longer visible.

The young princes paused to consider their predicament. "We must use our swords," Josiah said to Selwyn, "We can cut our way through these thorny obstacles that deter us. Once our way is clear, we can continue the search for Gilda." He drew the book from his doublet, changed it into his sword, and began to hack his way through the thorny brambles.

The brambles were tough and progress was slow. Josiah swung his sword with all his might, slashing at the dense thorns blocking his way. It was as though the brambles had a mind of their own and had decided that he should not be allowed to pass that way. The thorny branches seemed to reach for him, grabbing at his cloak and the sleeves of his doublet, tearing at his hands and clawing at his face. No sooner had he chopped them back than they reached out again like grasping hands, eager to grab and harm him. By the time he had advanced two or three paces through the brambles, the hilt of his sword was slippery with his own blood.

Gritting his teeth in determination, he gripped the sword

with both hands and worked even more furiously. Inch by inch, step by step, he fought his way forward through the relentless tangles of briars. His body was drenched with sweat; his breath came in ragged gasps.

The young prince hacked at a thick branch that blocked his path, watching in satisfaction as the shining blade of his sword sliced cleanly through it and allowed the branch to drop to the ground. In an instant, the branch grew back, again blocking his way and hindering his progress. He chopped it off a second time, and again, it immediately grew back. He turned, and to his horror, saw that the brambles behind him had grown back into place, completely surrounding him and cutting off his only avenue of escape. "Selwyn," he cried in desperation, "help me! These wretched brambles are growing back faster than I can cut them away!"

"I am here," came Selwyn's reply from a distance, "but I am battling the same brambles that you are."

"I am weary and my strength is gone," Josiah cried out. "I cannot fight any longer!"

"Fight in the strength of your King," Selwyn called. "His strength is your strength, and only in his strength can you prevail."

"Your Majesty," the young prince cried, holding his sword aloft with trembling hands, "I can no longer fight in my own strength! I must have your strength, or I am vanquished before I even reach Gilda's prison. It is for your honor and glory, my King, that I have set upon this quest! It is for the honor of your name, my Lord, that I seek to rescue Gilda and bring her back to the Castle of Faith."

Josiah swung the mighty sword with all of his strength, slashing and chopping at the relentless brambles that threatened him. The brambles grew faster and faster. Like a living creature with a thousand arms they closed in around him. Though he continued to cut them back, hacking away with a desperate strength, he could clearly see that he was losing the battle. He simply could not cut them back fast enough to keep them from engulfing him.

At once they were upon him, wrapping their deadly branches around his arms and legs like so many fiendish tentacles, lifting him off his feet and thrusting him backwards as if upon a wave of the ocean. Their strength was incredible and they gripped his hands so tightly that he could no longer wield his sword.

In desperation the young prince managed to pull the weapon close to him, holding it tightly against his side. When it transformed into the book he opened the cover, allowing the parchment to slip out. Unable to write a message or even to roll the petition into a scroll, he simply crumpled it in his hand and released it. To his immense relief, the crumpled parchment shot from his fingers and he knew that his wordless petition would instantly find its way to the throne room of Emmanuel.

The brambles continued to assault him, wrapping themselves around his neck and body until he could scarcely move. One deadly tentacle encompassed his neck and commenced to tighten around him in an attempt to strangle him. Helpless to fight back, he could only wait. Unless Emmanuel sent help, he was doomed.

He heard a crackling, popping sound and suddenly smelled smoke. The brambles loosened their hold on him and then began to recede. Relieved, he pulled his arms free of the encircling branches and then removed the one from around his neck. He turned and realized that he faced a new danger. The brambles were on fire!

An amber wall of flame swept across the glen, popping and snapping and devouring the tangles of deadly brambles like a hungry beast. With a roar, the fire swept toward Josiah. The heat was intense. Fear paralyzed him. Trapped by the menacing brambles, he was helpless to flee from the fire! He held his breath and waited.

To his amazement, the blaze abruptly died out just as it reached him. One instant he was facing a wall of flame more than ten feet high; in the next, the fire had simply disappeared. All that remained was a blackened path before him three or four yards wide. The flames had prepared a way of escape from the entangling brambles.

Prince Josiah leaped to his feet and hurried through the opening. In a moment he had left the glen and the brambles behind and was hurrying upward along a winding path through the forest. He looked around. Selwyn was not in sight. A golden beam of sunlight splashed across the trail, lifting his spirits and helping him to forget the horrors of the encounter with the brambles. He and Selwyn would continue on with the quest. They would find Gilda and set her free, enabling her to return to the Castle of Faith.

"Josiah!" The cry was a shout of desperation. "Help me, Josiah!"

The young prince spun around to see that Selwyn was battling for his life. Like a thousand fiendish serpents bent on destroying him, the brambles had enclosed him and were attacking him with ruthless ferocity. Selwyn wielded his sword with both hands, slashing and chopping at the relentless brambles that threatened him. The brambles grew faster and faster. Weaving and bobbing erratically, they closed in around him. Though he continued to cut them back, hacking away with a desperate strength, Josiah could clearly see that he was losing the battle. Selwyn simply could not cut them back fast enough to keep them from engulfing him.

"Josiah!"

Josiah snatched his book open and grabbed the parchment from within its pages. Selwyn was in extreme peril and he had no time to write a message to King Emmanuel. He simply rolled the parchment up and hastily released it. The wordless petition shot from his hands. "Stand fast, Selwyn," he cried, "for help is on its way!"

At that moment he heard the familiar crackling, roaring sound and turned to see a snarling wall of flame sweep across the glen toward the struggling form of Selwyn. Selwyn cried out in fear. His cries of terror turned to exclamations of astonishment as the brambles released him and the fire abruptly died out.

He was panting with exhaustion as he joined Josiah on the trail. "That was the most terrifying trial I have ever experienced," he gasped. "I thought that those wretched brambles would be the death of me! But did you see the fire? It looked as though it would burn me alive, but then it stopped just before it reached me! How do you account for that?"

"His Majesty sent the fire to save you from the brambles," Josiah explained, "in response to my petition on your behalf."

"Thank you," Selwyn replied fervently. "I owe my life to you."

"Praise the name of Emmanuel, for he is the one who saved you."

The two princes surveyed the area, noting that more brambles lay ahead. "Look," Selwyn said, pointing. "What is that?"

On the far side of the valley, less than a furlong from where the young princes stood, a mass of greenery rose above the slope. Josiah studied the unusual formation. At last, he shrugged. "I don't know...just more brambles, I guess."

Selwyn shook his head. "There's something strange about them, Josiah. Look how the one edge runs in a perfectly straight line, almost like the edge of a wall. And look at the corner—doesn't that look like a tower? The whole thing looks like a castle—a castle made of brambles!"

"Whoever saw a castle made of brambles?" Josiah scoffed.

"Perhaps it's not a castle made of brambles; perhaps it's a castle overgrown with them."

Josiah was still skeptical. "I think your imagination is getting the best of you again."

Selwyn edged toward the unusual formation and Josiah felt compelled to follow. "It's a castle of some sort, Josiah—it has to be! I can see the shape of the outer curtain, and the gatehouse, and... Look, Josiah! Look. It's a tower. This is the castle, Josiah! It has to be."

Josiah looked in the direction Selwyn was pointing so excitedly and saw a gray form rising above the mass of brambles. "It's a tower!" Selwyn declared again. "Josiah, this is the castle. It has to be!"

Josiah studied the structure. "Let's get closer."

The two princes moved cautiously to within fifty paces of the formation. Both studied the gray projection rising above the tangled mass of brambles. "You're right," Josiah said. "It *is* a castle! But how do we get in?"

Chapter Ten

Walking slowly and cautiously, Prince Josiah and Prince Selwyn advanced with swords drawn toward the bramble-covered castle. The drawbridge was down, but it was obscured by dense stands of brambles, and the main gate was not even discernible. Hacking away with all their might, they managed to cross the drawbridge and approach the main gate. Josiah cleared the dense foliage away from the entrance.

"Look," he told Selwyn, "I have found the portcullis. There is no longer any question—this is a castle! Perhaps this is where Gilda was taken."

Using his sword, Selwyn reached through the grating of the portcullis and cleared away some of the brambles. After a moment, he paused and studied the entrance. "I don't think this is the right castle, Josiah."

Josiah felt a surge of disappointment. "Why do you say that? This is the region where the innkeeper said it would be."

"I don't think anyone has entered this castle in the last ten years," Selwyn explained. "Look at all the brambles blocking the entrance. And take a look at the hinges on this gate— they're rusted tight. There's no one in this castle. It's been abandoned for years and years."

Selwyn's words brought a sinking feeling to Josiah's heart. "Then where is Gilda, if she's not here?"

Stepping back from the gate, Josiah raised his voice and shouted, "Gilda! Gilda, are you here?"

"Here? Here? Here?" the forest echoed, mocking him.

"Gilda! Where are you?"

"Are you? Are you? Are you?" the echo replied.

"Gilda! Are you here?"

"Here? Here? Here?"

The young prince eyed the lone tower that protruded from the brambles. "What if she's up in that tower, Selwyn?"

Selwyn studied the tower. "Don't you think she'd answer if she was?"

Josiah thought about it and then nodded reluctantly.

"Come on, Josiah, let's go home."

High in the castle tower, Gilda lay sleeping fitfully. Her mind was restless and her sleep was troubled by one terrifying dream after another. At one point she began to dream that she was being chased by Lady Acrimonious, who held a long, sharp dagger and was determined to kill her. Gilda struggled to run, but it seemed that her feet were made of stone. Her heart pounded with terror.

She heard a familiar sound and turned toward it. She stopped, listening intently, certain that she had heard someone calling her name.

"Gilda! Where are you?"

There it was again! The sound was very distant and indistinct, but she was sure that she had heard her name. She paused, heart pounding, and listened intently, but all she heard were the usual noises of the forest and the sounds of Lady Acrimonious in pursuit. She turned away.

"Gilda! Are you here?"

The voice was still far away, muffled and indistinct as if her name was being shouted from a great distance, but there was no mistake—someone was calling her. She gasped as she recognized the voice. It was Josiah. Her husband was calling her.

Gilda turned to flee toward the voice, but her feet refused to obey. She couldn't move. Taking a deep breath, she tried to call to Josiah, but found that she had no voice. She tried and tried to shout Josiah's name, struggling with all that was within her, but no sound came out. Her voice refused to respond. Tears welled up within her and spilled down her cheeks.

Her eyes opened and she stared groggily at her surroundings. Cold stone walls... a dark, circular chamber... a decaying ceiling above her head—where was she? Suddenly, memory sharpened and she knew: she was in the tower of Mara's castle. Sitting up, she disentangled her legs and feet from the coverlet and leaped from the bed. Dashing to the tower door, she grasped the handle and shook it fiercely, but it refused to budge. Just as she had feared, she was locked in.

Remembering the voice, she dashed to the one narrow window. She shuddered with disgust as she cleared the cobwebs away with one hand and then peered out. But the forest was dark and shadowy and she could see nothing. "Josiah?" she called softly, hesitantly. "Is that you? Josiah?"

But there was no answer. Stumbling back to the bed, she dropped onto it in a crumpled heap. *He doesn't really love you,* a voice within seemed to say, and Gilda raised her head to see if someone was in the solar with her. But there was no one. *He doesn't love you any more than Emmanuel does. He didn't come seeking you—it was just your imagination. You are alone... alone...*

alone... and no one really cares about you! Dropping her head, the princess began to weep bitterly.

The two princes hiked along a narrow trail as they hurried back to their horses. "This is where we fought the brambles," Selwyn observed, "but they don't seem to be resisting us now. I wonder why."

Josiah's mind was still on the mysterious, bramble-covered castle. "What if Gilda is in that tower?" he mused aloud. "Or what if she's in another part of the castle?"

"No one has gone in or out of that castle in the last ten years," Selwyn retorted. "You saw how the main gate was overgrown with brambles. The entire castle is!"

"These are not ordinary brambles," Prince Josiah replied. "They fought us as if they were determined to keep us from the castle, remember? What if they grew around the castle entrance just to keep us out?"

Selwyn turned and looked at him questioningly. "You mean in just a few minutes?"

Josiah nodded. "Perhaps. Ordinary brambles might have taken years to grow that tall and that thick, but these are no ordinary brambles. I don't think we can surmise that no one has entered the castle recently just because of the brambles."

"Did you see the rust on the gate hinges?" Selwyn asked. "They haven't been opened in years and years."

"Again, I think you're making an assumption," Josiah replied. He stopped in the middle of the trail and held up his hands. "Gilda may be in that castle. Selwyn, I want to go back."

"There was no sign of life anywhere around the castle," Selwyn argued. "Gilda's not there, Josiah."

"How do we know?" Josiah persisted. "The innkeeper identified the woman as Lady Acrimonious, and he told us that this was her castle. If she's the one who took Gilda, doesn't it make sense that Gilda would be in her castle?"

"We don't know for sure that we were at the right castle."

"It has to be. We followed the innkeeper's directions rather carefully."

"Until we were attacked by the brambles. Maybe that threw us off course and we ended up at the wrong castle."

Josiah shook his head. "I want to go back, Selwyn."

"We'd just be wasting our time."

"Gilda is my wife, Selwyn. If there is the slightest chance she's a prisoner in that castle, I want to find her."

"She's my sister, Josiah, but I just don't think she was there."

"I want to check it out."

"You called several times," Selwyn argued. "Don't you think Gilda would have answered if she was anywhere near the castle?"

"Perhaps she couldn't hear me. Or perhaps something or someone prevented her from answering."

Selwyn gave his brother-in-law a pleading look. "Let's go back to the Castle of Faith and talk it over with Sir Faithful," he suggested. "We could even bring him back to the bramble castle if he thinks it's worth checking."

"I'm going back," Josiah said firmly. "Now."

Selwyn shrugged. "As you wish. I'll go back to the Castle of Faith and talk with Sir Faithful. If he thinks Gilda might be at the castle, perhaps he would have Sir Watchful bring a garrison of knights."

"Send a petition to King Emmanuel for me," Josiah said. "I'm not sure how to get into the bramble castle, and I'm not sure what I'll find if I do get in."

"I will," Selwyn promised. "Be careful, Josiah."

Prince Josiah's heart pounded with anticipation as he approached the forbidding castle hidden in the brambles. One part of him wanted to flee in terror while another part thrilled at the idea of finding Gilda. The wind howled like a tormented spirit, moaning and groaning in the trees and flinging drops of rain into Josiah's face as if it resented his presence. The skies were dark and the castle seemed to glow with an unearthly greenish light. Lightning slashed across the sky and thunder boomed angrily in reply. Fear gripped Josiah's heart.

He drew his sword as he stepped onto the decaying draw-bridge. His footsteps on the rotting timbers sounded hollow-ly in the moat below, echoing and re-echoing with a strange rhythm that made him think of a beating heart. He paused long enough to send a petition to King Emmanuel.

Using his sword, he cleared most of the brambles from the portcullis and the main gate, half expecting that the tangled vegetation would grow back immediately. To his surprise, it did not. *How am I going to raise the portcullis?* he thought in dismay. *It must weigh tons! And how will I open the main gate?*

"Use the Key of Faith," a small voice said, and he looked up in surprise to see a snowy white dove perched on a branch extending over the castle wall.

"Aye," he said meekly. "I should have remembered."

Transforming his sword into the book, he opened the cov-er and removed a small golden key. Not knowing what else to do, he simply touched the key to the portcullis. With the groan of protesting pulleys and the rattle of heavy chains, the iron barrier slowly began to rise of its own accord.

Josiah stepped forward and ducked beneath the moving portcullis. *If it opened the portcullis, it ought to open the main gate as well,* he told himself. He touched the Key of Faith to the gate, which opened immediately with the protesting groan of rusty hinges.

The barbican was dark and gloomy, and Josiah's heart constricted with fear. Trembling, he swung the book to transform it into the sword. He passed through the main gate and into the barbican, moving slowly and cautiously and scanning each shadowy nook and cranny for any sign of opposition. But the barbican appeared to be empty and the only sounds he heard were the wail of the wind in the towers and the pounding of his own heart.

He began to relax. His thoughts turned to Gilda. *Will I find her here in the castle tower? Is she all right?*

Josiah passed through the inner gate and entered the bailey of the castle. He paused and surveyed the bailey, noting that dense brambles grew profusely along the walls, nearly obscuring the windows and doorways and completely covering the trees and shrubbery. A mound of brambles nearby turned out to be the castle well. But for the most part, the courtyard was clear, and he crossed it without incident.

Spotting an opening in the brambles on the far side of the bailey, he hurried toward it. He glanced behind him to make sure that he was not being followed and then stepped through a doorway into a musty, dimly-lit corridor. He held his sword against his side until it transformed into the book and then opened its pages to allow its light to illuminate the corridor.

He gasped in alarm. Standing to one side of the corridor was an enormous knight with a huge broadsword in his hands. There was no doubt whose side the knight was on; emblazoned across his breastplate was Argamor's coat of arms.

Josiah turned to run, but his feet seemed rooted to the spot. His legs began to shake, and the blood pounded in his head. His breath came in short, rapid gasps. He turned back toward the dark knight and then laughed in relief. The knight hadn't moved—he was nothing more than an empty suit of armor!

Stepping close to the suit of armor, the young prince rapped sharply on the breastplate with one gauntleted fist. "I hope I won't have to battle the knight who owns you," he told the armor. "He must be at least a foot taller than me."

Taking a deep breath, Josiah strode quickly down the corridor with the glow from the pages of the book lighting his way. He heard a slight sound and froze in his tracks, listening intently, not daring to move. Footsteps sounded in the corridor behind him and his heart constricted in fear. Someone or something was following him!

Hardly daring to breathe, he turned to look behind him.

"Arrgh!" His cry of alarm echoed throughout the castle. The dark knight that he had mistaken for an empty suit of armor now loomed over him with his enormous broadsword raised!

Josiah leaped backward, stumbling over his own feet and crashing to the floor in the process. Swinging his book, he transformed it into the sword just in time to repel a mighty blow from the enemy's sword.

He rolled clear and leaped to his feet. The huge knight took a step forward, brandishing the deadly broadsword with both hands. "For Emmanuel and for Gilda!" Josiah cried as he leaped forward to do battle with the dark knight.

The sounds of the conflict echoed up and down the dark corridor. Josiah soon found out that he was battling a fierce adversary. The dark knight's sword was swift; his strength was enormous; and he seemed to anticipate every move of Josiah's sword before he made it. "Your defeat is already accomplished!" the young prince cried, and his voice filled the corridor, echoing and re-echoing until it crescendoed like thunder. "I battle in the name of His Majesty, King Emmanuel, and with the sword given me by His Majesty. Your defeat is certain, dark knight!"

But the dark knight was silent. His only reply was a stunning blow from the broadsword that sent Josiah reeling.

"Help me, my Lord!" Josiah cried in alarm, "for I cannot send a petition!"

At that moment, a fiery streak of light flashed across the darkness of the corridor as the huge broadsword seemed to leap from the dark knight's hands to slam against the wall and then drop to the floor. His helmet tumbled from his shoulders to land upon the floor with a deafening clatter and his armor seemed to explode—greaves and vambraces and couters and gauntlets went flying through the air to clatter upon the floor beside the helmet.

Josiah stared in astonishment. The armor was empty; there was no knight inside.

With a huge grin of satisfaction upon his handsome features, Olympas returned his fiery sword to its sheath and then turned to his companion, a shining warrior nearly as tall as he. "Selwyn sent a petition on Josiah's behalf," he explained. Glancing with a look of disdain at the battered armor upon the floor, he followed Josiah down the corridor.

Suddenly the passageway before Josiah was filled with grotesque shadows that moved and undulated and continuously changed shape. Hateful voices filled the air. "Go back, foolish prince," they whispered in harsh, grating voices. "Go back, for your quest will end in failure. Gilda is lost—lost forever! There is nothing you can do to help her."

"Return to the Castle of Faith at once," another hateful voice demanded. "You are a trespasser, and you have no business here. Get out before we crush you like a worm."

"Get out! Get out!" The voices were becoming louder, harsher, more insistent. "Get out before we destroy you!"

"I have come in the name of His Majesty, King Emmanuel," Josiah replied, trying to keep his voice from trembling. "I come in his name and upon his authority."

"How can you speak the name of Emmanuel?" a mocking, gloating voice demanded. "Do you not realize what he has done to you? Where is your son, Ethan? Was he not taken by Emmanuel? Why do you serve a tyrant such as him?"

Glowing phantoms began to materialize in the corridor. Pale, translucent forms floated in the air above Josiah's head: leering old men; toothless, cackling hags; mocking, scornful children; all pointing accusingly at the terrified young prince as they glided slowly toward him and then vanished like vapors. Dark horsemen on glowing black chargers thundered through the corridor, throwing sparks from the hooves of their steeds as they rode down upon Josiah. Dark knights with swords drawn, huge dragons belching fire, hideous monsters with enormous fangs—the apparitions in the castle corridor came at him fast and furiously, overwhelming his senses and striking cold terror within him. Overcome with horror, he turned to flee.

He felt the pressure of a firm but gentle hand upon his shoulder, stopping him, turning him to face the horrors in the passageway. Shrieks of terror filled the corridor as the phantoms literally fell apart before his eyes to rain down upon the floor like pieces of shattered glassware. Josiah heard the sound of a sword being returned to a sheath. He turned, but saw no one in the corridor with him.

Several minutes later, after searching countless passageways and chambers within the gloomy castle, Josiah opened a narrow door to find himself outside on a bramble-covered balcony. His heart leaped. Directly in front of him was the single tower that rose above the rest of the castle! A narrow window near the top of the tower was not more than twenty feet above him.

"Gilda!" he called. "Gilda, are you there?" His voice echoed across the courtyard below.

Joy cascaded throughout his soul as a familiar face appeared at the window. "Gilda!"

A puzzled look appeared on Gilda's face as she scanned the courtyard and then the look was replaced by a look of surprise as she spotted Josiah. "What are you doing here?"

Josiah was overjoyed. "Gilda! Praise the name of Emmanuel; I have found you!"

An expression of annoyance crossed her face. "Why did you come here? I asked you not to follow me!"

"Gilda, I've come to take you home!"

The princess sighed. "I—I cannot return to the Castle of Faith, Josiah."

"I have come to get you out," Josiah replied. "I will take you back home to the Castle of Faith."

"I cannot come with you, Josiah. I—I cannot serve Emmanuel anymore."

"But you must," Josiah reasoned, looking up at her and trying to figure out how to get to the tower. "The only other choice is to serve Argamor!"

"I will not serve Argamor," Gilda replied, "but I cannot serve Emmanuel, either. You of all people should know how deeply the King has hurt me. Please, Josiah, return to the Castle of Faith without me."

"I cannot," the young prince replied. "I cannot live without you, Gilda." He leaned forward on the balcony, extending one hand as far as he could as if to be as close as possible to her. "Our King loves us, Gilda, loves us more than we can ever comprehend. I do not understand his entire plan for us, my love, but we must trust him. Come with me, Gilda, back to the Castle of Faith."

"I will always love you, Josiah, but I cannot return to the castle. You must go without me." With these words, she disappeared from the window.

"Gilda! Gilda, please! Come back!"

But the window was empty.

Twenty minutes later, after searching through the confusing maze of countless passageways, chambers, and tunnels, Josiah found the narrow, spiraling stairs that led to the top of the tower. His heart pounded with anticipation as he began to climb. Within moments he would rescue Gilda and return with her to the Castle of Faith!

Surprised at how quickly and easily he reached the top of the tower, he paused as he came to a locked door. His hands trembled as he opened his book and took out the Key of Faith. The door opened easily, and he rushed into a tiny solar containing a bed and an ancient spinning wheel. "Gilda!"

But the solar was empty. Gilda was not there.

Chapter Eleven

Darkness stole swiftly across the kingdom of Terrestria as Prince Josiah hiked wearily up a narrow trail. The young prince's steps were slow; his shoulders sagged; his face wore an expression of defeat. "How much farther to the Castle of Faith?" he wondered aloud. "I'm tired, cold, and hungry, and I'm not even sure that I'm heading in the right direction."

He paused, opened his book, and watched the pages for a moment to ascertain that he was indeed still traveling toward his home castle. Reassured, he returned the book to its place within his doublet. With a sigh, he resumed his weary trek.

What am I to do for my dear Gilda? he asked himself in despair. *I am sure that I have sent at least a hundred petitions to His Majesty on her behalf, and yet she is still the prisoner of that dread duchess. What am I to do for her?*

Darkness descended abruptly, and the creatures of the night filled the valley with a cacophony of assorted sounds. Josiah glanced around uneasily. "I'm not far from the Castle of Faith, but I may need a place to spend the night," he said aloud. His stomach growled with hunger and he sighed wistfully. "Oh, what I would give for a nice roast pheasant."

His attention was drawn to a pulsating amber glow just

ahead, and he hurried toward it. "Perhaps some kind stranger will share his campfire with me," he said aloud. He laughed in spite of his gloom. "And perhaps he has an extra roast pheasant on hand."

Moments later Josiah stepped into a clearing nestled between two wooded slopes. In the center of the clearing a cheerful fire leaped and danced with all its might. The fire was bounded by a ring of small boulders, and two forked sticks held a spit suspended over the crackling flames. To Josiah's delight, two golden brown pheasants were roasting upon the spit.

"I thought I was going to have to start without you, lad," a cheerful voice called. "The pheasants are just about done to perfection."

Startled, Josiah spun around. "Sir Wisdom!"

The nobleman strode briskly across the clearing and embraced the young prince. "Find a seat by the fire and get warm, my prince. Rest your weary feet. I'm serving brown bread, pheasant, and roasted apples, and it will all be ready in just a moment. We can talk as we dine."

Moments later Josiah took a bite of the roasted pheasant. "Excellent, Sir Wisdom, this is just excellent. You'll never know how much I needed this."

"I'm thankful that I can be of service," the old man said quietly. He studied the young prince. "What's on your heart, Josiah? I can tell that you are troubled, lad; it's written all over your face. Care to tell me what is wrong?"

Josiah took a refreshing drink from the flask that Sir Wisdom offered him. "Thank you, sire." He paused, not sure how to begin.

"I'm here to help, lad," the nobleman said gently.

Josiah nodded. "I know you are, sire, and I am grateful."

He let out his breath in a long sigh. "I don't think that I

can go on, sire. I have tried to be faithful and I have served Emmanuel with all my heart. But I'm not sure that I can do it any more."

"Not sure that you can serve King Emmanuel? What do you mean, Josiah?"

"I'm tired of being a knight, sire. I want to take my armor off and leave it off. I want to lay my sword down and never pick it up again. I don't want to face any more battles, or send any more petitions, or train any more young squires. Aye, I've had enough of knighthood."

"You're defeated and discouraged, my prince, but why? You're the son of His Majesty, King Emmanuel, Lord of Terrestria, and Lord of Eternity. Claim the victory that is rightfully yours as the heir to the kingdom."

"I've lost Ethan, sire, and now I've lost Gilda, and I know not how to rescue her. She says that she never wants to serve Emmanuel again, and I really don't know what to do to help her. As to being the son and heir of King Emmanuel, sire, I've waited for eleven years for King Emmanuel to return from the Golden City, and yet it's still not happened." The words came in a rush and Josiah almost felt a sense of relief when they were out.

He took another huge bite of roasted pheasant. "And now Argamor's troops are assembling in a secluded valley and it appears that they are preparing to attack the Castle of Faith."

Sir Wisdom was silent for several long moments. "You know all about the Great War," he said at last.

Josiah nodded. "Argamor has tried for centuries to seize His Majesty's throne and become the King of Terrestria."

The nobleman handed the young prince a roasted apple. "Try these. They're delicious." He added a log to the fire and Josiah watched as thousands of sparks flew skyward like ambitious fireflies.

"We're about to turn the last page in Terrestria's history," Sir Wisdom told Josiah, "and King Emmanuel's return from the Golden City is imminent. The final battle in the Great War is about to commence, and Gilda will play a major role in that battle."

Josiah was stunned. "Gilda? Why Gilda?"

Sir Wisdom hesitated. "Perhaps I should not tell you this." He watched the dancing flames of the campfire for a moment or two. "But I will. If Argamor can destroy Gilda with bitterness, he can use that victory to defeat one of Emmanuel's most valiant warriors."

"I—I don't understand," Josiah stammered. "How could Gilda's plight cause the defeat of a great warrior? Who is that warrior?"

Sir Wisdom turned and gazed intently at him. "You."

The young prince laughed in bewilderment. "Me? Surely you jest, sire. I am no great warrior."

"Your faithfulness in sending petitions to Emmanuel is the only power keeping Argamor from taking the Castle of Faith," Sir Wisdom replied soberly. "In taking your wife captive in hopes of destroying her with bitterness, Argamor plans to defeat you to cause you to cease sending petitions."

Josiah was stunned.

"In reality, the Great War is raging within Gilda's heart," the nobleman said. "Part of her wants to love and serve King Emmanuel, while part of her is being eaten up with bitterness and wants to renounce him forever."

"What am I to do, sire?"

"Send petitions on Gilda's behalf. Continue to send petitions on behalf of the Castle of Faith, for therein lies the strength of the castle. Without the petitions, the castle is doomed."

"Perhaps the castle is doomed anyway, with or without my petitions."

"Why do you say that, my prince?"

"Less than a mile from here is a secluded valley where Argamor's forces are gathering," Josiah told Sir Wisdom. "I passed by it just moments ago, sire. Their campfires extend across the valley for more than a mile. There must be thousands of troops there now! They have six or eight catapults and three or four trebuchets, and it's obvious that they're preparing for an assault on a castle or castles. Sire, the Castle of Faith is the closest to their campsite!"

"Then it is imperative that you continue to petition His Majesty for the protection of the castle," the nobleman told him.

Josiah sighed. "I'm not certain that my petitions are doing any good," he replied.

"What do you mean, Josiah?"

"I sent petitions on behalf of my son, yet King Emmanuel took him from us. I have petitioned Emmanuel repeatedly for Gilda, yet she remains a prisoner of this Lady Acrimonious and I know not where to find her. I have sent countless petitions on behalf of the Castle of Faith, yet right now there is an enemy force gathering that can wipe the castle off the face of Terrestria. Sire, it seems that my petitions are accomplishing nothing! His Majesty is not listening to me."

He took another drink from the flask. "We have been told that King Emmanuel will win the final battle in the Great War for Terrestria, right?"

Sir Wisdom nodded. "Of course. Emmanuel is Lord of Terrestria and always will be."

Prince Josiah hesitated. "Sire, it seems that Argamor is winning the battle!"

Sir Wisdom stirred the embers of the fire. "Go on."

"Certain magistrates are telling us that we must not display

King Emmanuel's coat of arms within the villages, lest some of the peasants be offended. Evil is flourishing throughout the kingdom. And right now a huge force of dark knights is assembling in a valley not more than five miles from my castle. If they attack the Castle of Faith—as it looks like they are planning to do—the castle and everyone in it will be destroyed! Sire, is Emmanuel not powerful enough to defeat Argamor's forces?"

The old nobleman studied Josiah for several long moments without speaking. Josiah grew uncomfortable under his gaze. At last, he spoke. "My prince, let's finish our dinner and then get some sleep," he said quietly. "Tomorrow you and I will take a little journey, for I want you to see firsthand the incredible power of your King, and just how the final battle of the Great War will come out."

Chapter Twelve

Josiah and Sir Wisdom followed the road as it descended a gentle slope. Josiah stopped and stared in wonder. "Oh, my!"

Before them lay a quiet valley, bright with life and promise. To the right of the road was a thriving apple orchard with branches so laden with fruit that the trees sagged under the weight. Wildflowers grew in colorful abundance to the left of the road; their fragrance wafted in the breezes like the essence of life. A crystal-clear brook laughed merrily as it crossed the roadway beneath a stone bridge and then meandered through acres and acres of brilliant blue flowers. Thousands of yellow butterflies danced in the air.

In the very center of the beautiful valley stood a castle of the purest white stone. A rainbow with seven colors hung over the castle, bold and brilliant against the deep blue of the cloudless sky.

"It's the rainbow of promise!" Josiah breathed. He looked in bewilderment at his companion. "The Castle of Knowledge? You brought me to the Castle of Knowledge?"

"We're going to visit the Library of Learning that you might see just what your King has planned for Terrestria," Sir Wisdom replied. "Once you see for yourself just what Emmanuel is going to do, I think your heart will be encouraged."

He strode forward. "Come on, Student is waiting for us."

The drawbridge was down and the portcullis was up, so Josiah and Sir Wisdom stepped boldly onto the drawbridge to be met by a knight in white armor. "Identify yourselves, my lords," the knight requested pleasantly.

"I am Prince Josiah of the Castle of Faith, royal heir to King Emmanuel, and with me is an old friend, Sir Wisdom. We are here to visit the Library of Learning."

The guard stepped to one side. "Enter, my lords, and may your stay at the castle be a pleasant one."

A young man of slender build hurried forward to greet them, adjusting his spectacles and flashing a friendly smile as he entered the gatehouse. "Welcome back to the Castle of Knowledge, Prince Josiah! It is an honor to have you visit the castle once again."

"Indeed it is an honor to be here once again, Student," Josiah replied. "Ever since I stopped here while on my quest for the seven castles, I have longed to return as often as possible."

"Aye, we have been expecting you," the enthusiastic man told him. "We are delighted that you are here." Behind the round lenses of his spectacles, Student's eyes sparkled with an intensity that told Josiah that his host meant every word. "As before, my purpose is to assist you in obtaining a deeper, fuller knowledge of your King." His eyes seemed to glow as he said, "The more that one learns of His Majesty, the more one loves him."

Together Josiah, Sir Wisdom, and the castle steward strolled through a tiny courtyard alive with flowering trees and colorful flower gardens. A small spring bubbled up in the center of the courtyard; the crystal-clear water flowed along a rock-lined channel and disappeared beneath the wall at the opposite end.

"Your solar is ready in the east tower, should you desire to spend the night," Student said, pointing toward the upper corner of the castle wall, "but first I will take you to the Library of Learning."

Josiah and Sir Wisdom followed him through a doorway and then paused in reverence. The three men were standing on the polished marble floor of a room so immense that Josiah could not see the far end. There was no furniture in the vast room; but the walls were adorned with enormous, gilt-framed paintings that reached from floor to ceiling. Josiah shook his head in bewilderment. The library appeared to be a hundred times larger than the entire Castle of Knowledge! How could such a huge library fit within such a tiny castle?

"As before, you are welcome to visit any or all of the books," Student invited quietly. "As you remember, there are sixty-six volumes." He gestured toward the nearest wall. "The paintings that you see are in reality volumes of wisdom and instruction. Some give the history of Terrestria; others simply relate or explain His Majesty's edicts and commandments." He stepped closer to a huge picture that depicted a beautiful outdoor scene with purple mountains, a flowing river, and a luscious garden. As Josiah moved toward the painting, the scene was alive with movement—the river in the picture was actually flowing; the leaves on the trees fluttered in a gentle breeze; birds flew from branch to branch. The effect was that of looking through a window.

"We want to visit the last volume in the New Wing," Sir Wisdom told Student.

"Aye, the Book of the Apocalypse," the steward replied. "Are you wishing to study Emmanuel's plans for Terrestria?"

"That's exactly what we are after," the nobleman replied. "I want my young friend to witness for himself just how complete a victory His Majesty will accomplish."

Student turned to Josiah. "What you are about to see will absolutely overwhelm you," he promised. "One has no idea just how mighty His Majesty really is until he witnesses the events of the Apocalypse.

"Follow me," he told his guests. "The Book of the Apocalypse is in the New Wing of the library and you may explore it to your heart's content." The footsteps of the steward, the prince, and the nobleman echoed throughout the vast chamber as they walked across the Library of Learning.

After passing a number of the enormous paintings, the men stepped through a doorway covered by a thick veil and entered a second room nearly as large as the first. They crossed the room and then the steward paused before the last picture. Josiah stepped to the edge of the painting and peered in, and his heart pounded with the thrill of anticipation. He was standing at the brink of a broad, slow-moving river. Just beyond the beautiful river were the glistening walls and towers of the Golden City of the Redeemed!

Student laid a hand on Josiah's arm. "In this volume you will witness some events which are terrifying, but you will not be in any danger. You will observe a number of horrendous plagues and judgments that His Majesty will inflict upon the unbelieving peasants, but remember that none of these will fall upon his own children. Also remember, Prince Josiah, the inhabitants of the time that you are about to visit cannot see or hear you, nor will they be aware of your presence. You cannot speak to them, nor will they speak to you. You are merely an observer."

Sir Wisdom moved in beside him. "Well, my prince, are we ready? What you are about to see will impact you forever." He held out his hand. "May I see your book, if you please?"

Josiah drew the book from his doublet and handed it to the nobleman, who opened it to a particular passage and handed it back.

Josiah stepped closer to the base of the enormous picture. A thrill of excitement swept over him as he lifted his foot to step over the frame of the picture and into the Book of the Apocalypse.

In an instant, Sir Wisdom and Prince Josiah were standing on the battlements atop the inner curtain wall of a castle. The sounds of fierce conflict filled the air: the clash of swords, the twang of archers' bowstrings, the shouted commands of captains, the cries of wounded knights, and the heavy thud, thud, thud of a battering ram against a castle gate. Josiah realized that the castle residents were engaged in a desperate battle. He looked down from the battlements and gasped as he saw vast hordes of dark knights screaming with rage as they stormed the castle walls.

"There must be tens of thousands of the enemy!" he cried in alarm to Sir Wisdom. "The castle doesn't stand a chance!" Just then a huge boulder shot skyward to sail over the castle walls and crash through the roof of the castle great hall. Josiah winced. "They have one, two, three... six catapults, sire, and two trebuchets, and siege towers, and... Look, sire! There are peasants helping the dark knights storm the castle!"

"The peasants of Terrestria will side with Argamor in the final battles of the Great War," Sir Wisdom said quietly. "No one will be neutral."

As Josiah watched in horrified fascination, one of the siege towers moved close to the outer curtain wall of the castle. A ramp at the top of the tower dropped open to rest on the top of the wall and hordes of screaming dark knights and peasants rushed along the battlements to do battle with the archers defending the walls.

A crashing, splintering sound reverberated throughout the castle, and the main gate suddenly crashed open. A host of dark knights flooded through the gate, shouting the name of Argamor as they attacked the small contingent of knights who stood their ground and attempted to defend the castle entrance. "It's all over," Josiah moaned. "The enemy troops are within the castle!"

Sick at heart, the young prince watched in silence as the screaming, cursing hordes of peasants and dark knights continued to rush across the drawbridge and storm into the castle. Within moments, the barbican was filled with angry, cursing warriors. The swarming mass surged forward and began to attack the inner gate. A handful of Emmanuel's archers on the inner curtain wall sent a barrage of arrows into the barbican as they tried valiantly to pick off as many of the enemy as they could.

"I can't bear to watch," Josiah cried, burying his face in his hands. "The castle residents will be massacred! Sir Wisdom, isn't there something we can do?"

"We are merely observers," the nobleman said quietly, calmly. "We are here to see the future."

A horrendous thought occurred to Josiah and he lifted his head to look at Sir Wisdom. "Are Argamor's forces attacking all of Emmanuel's castles? All over Terrestria?"

His companion nodded.

"Including the Castle of Faith?"

Sir Wisdom nodded again.

Shouts of victory drew Josiah's attention down to the bailey, and in horror he realized that the swarms of dark knights had managed to open the inner gates and gain access to the bailey. His heart sank as he watched the cursing hordes of evil warriors flood into the courtyard. The castle residents fled in terror.

The sound of raucous cheering filled the barbican and the bailey and Josiah looked down to see the invaders celebrating. Calling the name of Argamor and cursing the name of Emmanuel, the dark knights and their peasant counterparts leaped about for joy, hurled their helmets and shields into the air, and ran about in frenzy. "I cannot bear to watch any longer!" Josiah cried, shutting his book. The castle vanished and once again, he and Sir Wisdom were standing within the Library of Learning.

Sir Wisdom had a strange look upon his countenance. "The peasants and the dark knights were celebrating what they see as a great victory," he said quietly.

"The defeat of King Emmanuel's castle?"

The nobleman nodded. "The peasants and the dark knights have hated Emmanuel's children, and they have hated the Castle of Faith, for they hate Emmanuel and they hate righteousness. To them, their victory today is cause for celebration and rejoicing."

He sighed. "Little do they realize that horrors will soon be upon them, bringing terrors far greater than their worst nightmares."

Chapter Thirteen

After opening the book again, Prince Josiah and Sir Wisdom approached the main gate of a noisy, bustling city. The roadway was filled with travelers: some on horses and donkeys, some riding in carriages and wagons and other conveyances, and many on foot. Well-dressed merchants bringing their goods into the city shouted greetings or insults to each other while peasant farmers worked the fields just outside the city walls. A lone shepherd attempted to guide a small flock of sheep through the city gate. The unpleasant sound of angry children quarreling was audible above the other noises of the busy city.

"This is the City of Worldly Pleasures," Sir Wisdom told Josiah. "The inhabitants of this vile place have spent their lives seeking frivolous pleasures, rather than serving the King who made them. Little do they know that the time of pleasure is about to end."

"What road is this?" Josiah asked.

"This is the King's Highway," Sir Wisdom replied, "also known as the Highway of Life. The highway was built by King Emmanuel, and it travels all the way across Terrestria. These people use it daily, but not one of them has taken the time to acknowledge Emmanuel's goodness to them in providing it."

"Pardon me, please." Josiah stepped around a tall, thin woman carrying two pails of water.

Sir Wisdom gripped his elbow. "The inhabitants of this land can neither see nor hear you, Josiah. You are a visitor from another dimension of time."

The young prince grinned sheepishly. "I forgot."

The nobleman guided him to one side of the King's Highway. "In the Golden City, His Majesty has just opened the first of seven seals. His judgments upon the peasants of Terrestria are about to commence." He took a seat upon a large boulder at the side of the highway and then indicated that Josiah was to do the same. "We can watch from here."

The clatter of a horse's hooves rang like a blacksmith's hammer across the moors, and an enormous white horse thundered into view, running hard along the King's Highway. His rider wore a golden crown and held a bow in his left hand, and his face was as stone. The townspeople screamed in fear at his sudden appearance, scattering left and right in a desperate attempt to get out of his way. The grim horseman reined in as he reached the city gate. Standing in the stirrups, he reached upward and made a slashing motion with one hand as though making an invisible mark above the gate. He then rode swiftly through the city. Terrified screams marked his route.

"The appearance of the white horse signifies that the time of judgment has come," Sir Wisdom said gravely. "Throughout the eons of time, Emmanuel has extended his grace to any and all who will come to him, but now that time has passed. Those who have not responded to his grace will now experience his wrath. It is indeed a fearful thing to fall into the hands of the living King."

As he spoke, a tremendous earthquake shook the ground. Cracks appeared in the city walls, and bits of mortar and stone fell to the ground. In the distance, the mountains swayed and trembled. The townspeople shrieked in terror. A team of horses bolted in panic, dashing along the highway and overturning the wagon they pulled. The driver was thrown against a tree. The sky became black and a howling wind snatched at Josiah's clothing while hot bolts of lightning slashed across the heavens. Thunder rumbled, and the cold hand of fear gripped Josiah's heart.

The sounds of another horse drew Josiah's attention back to the highway, and he turned to see a huge red horse thundering along in the unearthly twilight that prevailed. His rider carried an enormous sword, which he brandished as if riding into battle. "This rider will take peace from Terrestria," the nobleman told Josiah in hushed tones, "so that the inhabitants will begin to kill one another. Sad times are ahead for Terrestria, my prince."

Pandemonium prevailed at the appearance of the second horse. Screaming with terror, many of the townspeople ran for their lives while others dropped to the ground and cowered in horror. Donkeys brayed in fear. Dogs howled. As the second horseman rode through the city, the resulting chaos sounded like a desperate battle.

An enormous black horse rode swiftly into view, and Josiah noticed that his rider held a pair of balances in his hand. "A measure of wheat for a day's wages," cried a great voice, as if from the skies, "and three measures of barley for a day's wages, and see that you hurt not the oil and the wine." Eyes wide with unbelief and horror, most of the peasants now cowered in silence. A few sobbed or wailed aloud with fear. The horseman rode swiftly through the gate and disappeared into the city.

Josiah turned to his companion. "Who is this rider?" he asked. "What will he do?"

"He brings famine," Sir Wisdom replied sadly, "famine such as Terrestria has never seen. The crops will fail, and the people of Terrestria will starve. Lifelong friends and families will turn on each other in an attempt to get enough food to stay alive. As a result of the famine, the economy of Terrestria will be destroyed and commerce will cease."

After several minutes of unearthly silence, the stunned residents of the city began to gather in small groups, fearfully discussing the horrendous appearances that they had just witnessed. The trembling shepherd made an effort to gather his flock, which had scattered at the appearance of the first horseman.

Just then, a woman screamed. "Here comes another horseman!"

A fourth horse, pale and gaunt, galloped into view. His rider was dressed in solid black and his face was a death mask. Across his saddle he carried an enormous battleaxe. "Who is this horseman?" Josiah asked in a low voice that trembled with fear.

"His name is Death," Sir Wisdom answered gravely, "and he has been given the power to kill one-fourth of Terrestria's inhabitants with the sword, with hunger, with the beasts of the earth, and with death itself."

Josiah's heart pounded with dread as he watched the city's inhabitants, many of them prostrate with fear upon the ground while others wailed and sobbed. Still others sat upon the ground, eyes wide and staring, stunned into silence by the terrifying appearances of the four horsemen. "They really don't realize just what they are facing, do they?"

Sir Wisdom laid a hand upon his arm. "His Majesty's judgments have just begun," he replied quietly. "Only four seals have been opened, and there are three more yet to be opened. Far worse than this is yet to come."

At that moment, a strange clamoring filled the air. Josiah stopped and listened. It was as though thousands, perhaps millions, of voices were crying out, yet he could not understand what they were saying. He strained to hear, but could not understand the words. The voices became louder. At last, he could make out the words. "How long, Oh Lord, how long? How long before you avenge our blood on them that dwell in Terrestria?"

Josiah looked to Sir Wisdom for an explanation.

"The voices you hear are the souls of those who have been martyred for their faithfulness to Emanuel," he said. "The fifth seal has been opened."

A horrendous earthquake shook the ground just then. Those who were standing were knocked to the ground. Parts of the city wall broke loose and tumbled down. One of the gates twisted loose from its hinges and came crashing to the ground. Windows shattered. Trees on the hillside above the city danced and swayed.

A woman shrieked with terror. "Look! Look at the sun! It has become black as sackcloth of hair!"

"Look at the moon!" a man cried.

The moon, visible even though it was daytime, had become as red as blood. Josiah turned away in horror.

A blazing streak of intense light flashed across the heavens, striking the earth with such force that it shook the foundations of the city. Seconds later, another blazing object streaked across the skies to strike the hillside, setting fire to the forest. "Even the stars are falling," Sir Wisdom said in awe.

At that moment, the blue sky above their heads jerked violently to one side as if snatched away by a giant hand, leaving in its place a deep, empty blackness. The mountains trembled and shook.

As Josiah and Sir Wisdom watched in silence, townspeople by the scores came dashing out of the city, running to the hills and crying, "Fall on us and hide us! Hide us from the face of Emmanuel, for the day of his wrath is come! Who shall be able to stand before his great wrath?"

"I cannot bear to watch any more!" Josiah cried to Sir Wisdom. With trembling hands he closed the book, and he and the nobleman found themselves standing on the polished marble floor of the vast Library of Learning.

"Six seals have been opened," Sir Wisdom said quietly, "but there is yet one more. When it is opened, seven trumpets will sound, bringing yet more judgment and anguish upon those peasants who chose to reject their King."

"This is the farm of Tobias," Sir Wisdom said, as he and Prince Josiah walked into the barnyard of a large, prosperous farm that sloped down to the edge of a sapphire blue sea. To the east was a thriving vineyard with vines groaning under the weight of huge clusters of luscious purple fruit; to the west stood shimmering fields of golden wheat ready for harvest. The nobleman led the young prince around behind the first of three large barns. "Tobias is a great man in these parts and has become quite wealthy. He has seven sons and three daughters."

"His vineyard is flourishing," Josiah commented, looking at the rows of vines where nearly a dozen women with large woven baskets were working, frantically picking the fruit from the vines. "Look at the size of those luscious grapes!

"And look at that healthy wheat crop," he said, glancing toward the fields where a score of men were working vigorously, swinging sickles with all their might as they harvested the grain. "Never before have I seen such wheat."

"The famine has not touched here yet," Sir Wisdom replied. "When it does, this farm will be one of the hardest hit."

As Josiah watched, a farm wagon loaded with wheat approached the nearest barn. A tall, broad-shouldered young man leaped down from the wagon and approached a man who was busily sharpening a sickle.

"The men cannot work any faster, Father," the younger man said. "They are about to drop from exhaustion. I simply cannot push them to work any harder."

"But you must, Simeon, you must!" the older man urged, but not unkindly. He glanced at the skies, which were dark and lowering. Thunder rumbled across the heavens, and lightning split the sky as a gusting wind shrieked and howled. "Son, never before have I seen weather like this at harvest time. Something dreadful is about to happen; I can feel it. Perhaps it has something to do with the four dreadful horsemen that we saw. But we simply must get the harvest in before it is destroyed."

A young woman approached just then. "Father, may I give the women a brief rest? Some of them look as if they are about to faint."

Tobias shook his head. "We must get the harvest in, Rhoda. If we lose it, we are ruined!"

A mighty trumpet blast reverberated across the skies, echoing and re-echoing across the vast expanses of the farm. Rhoda screamed and Simeon flinched, while Tobias looked questioningly at the sky. He frowned in bewilderment.

"The first trumpet has sounded," Sir Wisdom said quietly to Josiah.

Loud, sharp reports echoed across the skies like rapid claps of thunder, and huge hailstones came streaking from the darkened skies to strike the earth with tremendous force. Sheets of crimson flame flashed downward repeatedly as if the earth was being beaten with a giant torch.

Josiah turned to run to the safety of the barn, but Sir Wisdom grabbed his arm. "We are in no danger," he said quietly.

With shouts of alarm, the farmhands dropped their sickles and ran frantically for the barns while the women ran screaming from the vineyard. Trembling, they gathered around Tobias. A farmhand ran up to Simeon and talked with him briefly, gesturing wildly as he spoke.

"Father, at least a third of the wheat has been destroyed," Simeon reported.

"A large part of the vineyards have been destroyed also," Rhoda reported, sobbing. "Oh, Father, what is happening?"

Sir Wisdom stepped close to Josiah. "One third of the trees and vegetation in the kingdom have been destroyed," he said quietly, "as well as all grass."

Another mighty trumpet blast rang out just then, and some of the women screamed. Seconds later an enormous burning object fell from the skies to land in the sea with a mighty splash. A tidal wave taller than a mountain crashed down upon the lower edge of the wheat field and then flowed back down into the sea. While the others watched in horror, one brave farmhand dashed down to the edge of the farm and peered over the edge of a cliff.

His face was ashen when he returned. "One t-third of the s-sea has become b-blood," he stammered, "and thousands of fish and other creatures are floating in it, dead!"

Sir Wisdom leaned close to Josiah. "One third of the ships upon the seas of Terrestria have also been destroyed," he said quietly.

A third trumpet sounded just then, and a huge burning object streaked across the heavens and struck the earth just beyond the horizon. The impact shook the farm. "What was that?" a man cried.

"I do not know, and I probably don't want to find out," Tobias muttered.

Josiah looked to his companion for an explanation. "A star was cast from the heavens and struck the waters of Terrestria," the nobleman explained. "One third of the waters of the kingdom have been poisoned, and many will die."

Another trumpet sounded, and Rhoda began to sob. "What is happening, Father?" She clung to his arm.

Tobias cursed. "Emmanuel is destroying us, my child," he replied, shaking with fear. "We are all dead men!"

Rhoda wailed. "Will any of us live through this?"

"What is that, sire?" one of the servants cried, pointing.

As the terrified group watched in horrified silence, a wall of darkness swept across the wheat fields, moving steadily toward the barns like an approaching army. "What is it?" the servant cried again.

The darkness abruptly closed over the farmyard as if someone had pulled an enormous veil over the farm. All was silent except for the sound of someone sobbing. "What has happened?" Josiah asked Sir Wisdom.

"When the fourth trumpet sounded," the nobleman replied, "a third part of the sun and the moon were smitten. Darkness will prevail for one third of the day and also for one third of the night. With this unnatural darkness will come a terror that will drive men insane."

"Woe, woe, woe," cried a great voice, as if from the skies, "Woe to the inhabitants of Terrestria by reason of the other voices of the trumpets of the three shining ones, which are yet to sound!"

Another trumpet blast rang out across the darkened skies,

and Tobias cursed. "Emmanuel," he screamed, "we cannot take any more! Leave us alone! Leave us alone! We want nothing to do with you, wretched tyrant!"

Just then came a rumbling sound in the distance. The noise grew louder by the moment, as if the source of the sound was approaching the farm. Josiah gripped Sir Wisdom's arm. "It sounds like horses," he said in a husky voice. "Thousands and thousands and thousands of horses!"

"That which approaches is far worse than horses," the nobleman told him. "They are actually enormous locusts with the power of scorpions in their tails. Terrestria has never seen such horror as is now descending upon the kingdom."

As he spoke, a cloud of enormous creatures swooped down upon the farm. The air was filled with the sounds of horses and chariots rushing into battle. "They look like horses," cried a servant in terror, "but they have faces like men and hair like women!"

"They have the teeth of lions!" cried another.

"Run!" Tobias shouted. "Run for your lives!"

The group scattered in panic, some running for the safety of the farmhouse while others ran blindly toward the vineyards and the wheat fields. As Josiah watched in horror, the winged creatures swept down upon the fleeing Terrestrians. Each time a locust came in contact with a Terrestrian, that person fell screaming to the ground and writhed in pain. "What are they doing?" Josiah cried.

"They have stings in their tails," Sir Wisdom answered, "and can inflict pain such as a scorpion would inflict. This horror will be upon Terrestria for the next five months."

"Five months!" Josiah was aghast. "Will any of the peasants survive five months of this torture?"

"They will, though they will wish that they could die. In

fact, many will actively seek death, and yet it will be denied them." Sir Wisdom shook his head sadly. "This is only the first of the three great woes. The fifth trumpet has sounded, but there are yet two more."

Josiah gripped his arm. "We must leave this place," he begged. "I cannot bear to see any more at this time."

The nobleman nodded. "As you wish."

Josiah closed his book and experienced a huge sense of relief as he was surrounded by the beauty of the vast Library of Learning. To his amazement, he realized that he was weeping. "It is all too horrid," he sobbed. "How can any of the peasants live through these judgments?"

"They have brought these judgments upon themselves," his companion reminded him. "They have rejected His Majesty's offers of mercy and forgiveness, and in doing so, have brought judgment upon themselves."

Josiah nodded. "I know, and I know that King Emmanuel is just and right to bring these horrors upon them. But still, sire, it grieves me deeply to see what is going to happen to those who reject our King." He raised his head to look at Sir Wisdom with tear-filled eyes. "One part of me rejoices to know that those who hate Emmanuel will feel the power of his wrath, and yet, another part of me goes out to them in pity. Does that make sense?"

The nobleman nodded. "We must be diligent to encourage the peasants to receive Emmanuel's pardon for them in order that they might become his children. Those who do will escape the horrors of the judgments that we have just witnessed, but those who reject will experience the terrors of his wrath."

He gestured toward Josiah's book. "There is more that you must see. Are you ready?"

Josiah sighed deeply, took a deep breath, and opened the book.

Chapter Fourteen

Prince Josiah and Sir Wisdom found themselves standing on a hillside overlooking a vast, desolate valley. As they watched, great hordes of people swarmed into the valley from all directions. Within minutes, millions of Terrestrians filled the area like a living sea of humanity. Dark warriors and peasants alike, young and old, male and female, they stood eagerly watching as if awaiting some great event.

"What is happening here?" Josiah asked Sir Wisdom, but the nobleman shook his head.

"Just watch."

"Lords and ladies of the realm of darkness," a powerful voice thundered across the vast assembly, and Josiah turned to see a figure standing upon a high, jagged outcropping of red sandstone in the center of the valley. "Servants of His Lordship, the rightful King of Terrestria, I give you His Lordship, Lord Argamor!"

The vast throng of Terrestrians and dark knights leaped to their feet at the appearance of another figure atop the stone promontory. Cheering wildly, they leaped about in frenzy, making the vast valley ring with the sounds of their voices. Josiah inhaled sharply. "Argamor!"

"Lords and ladies of the realm of darkness," Argamor's powerful voice thundered across the vast throng, "we stand upon the threshold of the greatest period in the history of Terrestria! Soon and very soon we shall throw off the shackles of Emmanuel's tyrannical rule and we shall be free! Terrestria shall be ours!"

Wild screams and frenzied cheering greeted his words.

Shackles, Josiah thought. *How can he use the word 'shackles' when referring to His Majesty's rule? Argamor is the one who enslaves people with shackles; Emmanuel sets them free!* Eleven years earlier, young Josiah had languished in slavery to Argamor, hating the weight of guilt and the chain of iniquity fastened to his ankle, hating the loathsome Dungeon of Condemnation where he was imprisoned every night. His heart thrilled at the memory of the blessed day when King Emmanuel had arrived in the Coach of Grace and set him free forever.

"My lords and my ladies," Argamor continued, when the wild cheering had subsided somewhat, "do not be intimidated by Emmanuel's feeble display of power upon Terrestria in recent days. His intention is to frighten you into submission, but do not be alarmed—we shall prevail." He paused and scanned the audience to see what effect his words were having.

"This place is a natural amphitheater," Josiah told Sir Wisdom. "We can hear every word."

"Today is a great moment in the history of Terrestria," the powerful warlord continued, "for today brings the coronation of a new leader, the great and mighty Alphaomega. Bow before him, my loyal followers, for today he stands before you as your King. Today Emmanuel's tyrannical rule comes to an abrupt end as King Alphaomega takes the throne!"

As these words were spoken a figure made his way to the top of the promontory and stood before Argamor, who placed a golden crown upon his head and a regal crimson robe around his shoulders. The cheers from the crowd were deafening.

"Alphaomega," Josiah repeated, turning to Sir Wisdom. "Isn't that one of His Majesty's names?"

"Actually it is one of his titles, and it means 'the first and the last,' signifying that His Majesty is Lord of Eternity. In claiming this title as his name, Argamor has clearly marked this 'Alphaomega' as a usurper of King Emmanuel's throne."

Josiah's gaze swept across the vast throng of Terrestrian peasants and dark warriors, all of whom were kneeling before the newly acclaimed leader. "They have accepted him as their lord," he observed quietly. "Without exception, every man, woman, and child is bowing before him."

"There are many in Terrestria who will not bow to this man or his image," Sir Wisdom told him, "but they are not here today."

"My loyal subjects," Alphaomega began, speaking in a powerful, captivating voice that made the dark skies above him ring with the sound of his words, "thank you for your attendance at this grand moment in our history. The governors and rulers and magistrates of Terrestria have pledged me their power and their loyalty, and I ask you to do the same. United as one, together we shall break the chains of Emmanuel's tyranny forever, thus establishing ourselves as the true rulers of Terrestria and masters of our own fate! My lords and my ladies, are you ready to rule Terrestria?"

In answer, the vast throng leaped to their feet and began to shout the name of their new leader. "Alphaomega! Alphaomega! Alphaomega!"

"How like Argamor," Sir Wisdom growled in disgust, "to promise these people power and freedom in order to enslave them and claim the power for himself."

"What will this new leader do?" Josiah asked.

"Close your book and let's go back to the library to discuss it," the nobleman replied. "This valley is a place of intense evil."

Moments later the two stood before the huge painting which was the Book of the Apocalypse. "So who is this Alphaomega person?" Josiah questioned. "And why is Argamor putting him in charge? I cannot imagine Argamor sharing his power with anyone."

"Argamor is setting Alphaomega up as the False King in an attempt to bring all of Terrestria together to fight against Emmanuel. You heard what Alphaomega told the people: the governors and rulers and magistrates of Terrestria have pledged their loyalty and power to him. In uniting all the governors and rulers of Terrestria into one government, Argamor hopes to gain the power to seize His Majesty's throne.

"In addition to establishing a False King, Argamor also plans to give power to a False Prophet. The man will have incredible powers, so that he can even call fire down from the skies. This False Prophet will direct the people to build a gigantic image of Alphaomega, and he will dictate that they are to worship him and the image. He will actually have the power to cause the image of Alphaomega to move and speak, and anyone who will not worship the image will be killed.

"He will also cause everyone to receive a special mark in their hand or their forehead as a symbol of their allegiance to the False King. No one will be allowed to buy or sell anything without having that mark."

"What is the mark?"

"Actually, it is a number. The number is six hundred sixty-six."

Josiah was silent for several moments as he thought it

through. "How will it all end?" he finally asked. "When will King Emmanuel come back to Terrestria and establish his eternal kingdom?"

"The answers, of course," Sir Wisdom said with a smile, "are in your book. I could simply tell you, but let's go back into the Book of the Apocalypse that you might see for yourself."

Prince Josiah and Sir Wisdom stood on the pinnacle of a great and mighty mountain. Much of Terrestria was visible from this great height. To the west was the Great City where the False King had established his throne, and just beyond, a great sea. To the east of the mountain flowed a majestic river.

"Please allow me to see your book," the nobleman requested. When Josiah handed it to him, he glanced at the open page and handed it back. "The seventh trumpet has just sounded," he told the young prince, "and seven mighty vials of judgment are about to be poured out upon Terrestria. When the seventh vial has been poured out, the greatest battle in all of Terrestria's history will commence. We are about to see an incredible display of His Majesty's power."

As he spoke, a mighty shining warrior descended from the skies holding a large golden vessel in his hands. The warrior tipped the huge vessel, allowing a fiery red liquid to cascade down upon the earth. Immediately, cries of pain and of rage were audible from the inhabitants of the Great City.

"What happened?" Josiah questioned.

"The first vial has caused grievous sores upon all those who have received the mark of the False King and upon all those who have worshipped his image."

"Those within the Great City?"

"Anyone anywhere in Terrestria," the nobleman answered.

A second shining warrior flew across the skies with a second great golden vessel. Hovering on mighty wings above the sea, he emptied his vial into the waters. "What did that do?" Josiah asked.

"It will cause all the living creatures in all the seas of Terrestria to die," Sir Wisdom replied.

A third great warrior emptied a great golden vessel upon the rivers and fountains of Terrestria. "All the rivers and water sources within the kingdom have just become blood," Sir Wisdom said soberly.

"You are righteous, Oh Emmanuel, Master of Eternity," the shining warrior cried with a mighty voice that resonated across the skies, "because you have judged thus. They have shed the blood of your children and of your prophets, and you have given them blood to drink, for they are worthy."

Just then a fourth great shining warrior poured his huge golden vial upon the sun. As Josiah watched in wonder, the sun began to pulsate with incredible bursts of light and heat. "The sun has been given power to scorch the peasants with great heat," Sir Wisdom said quietly, "so great that in their pain they will blaspheme the name of Emmanuel."

Another shining warrior sped across the skies and quickly emptied his great golden vessel over the Great City. Josiah watched a dark liquid cascade down upon the city and then noticed that an unnatural darkness settled over the city. Cries of pain and agony rose from the streets. "This darkness is so intense that it causes excruciating pain," Sir Wisdom explained.

Josiah could see areas of darkness spreading throughout the kingdom. "Will this affect all of Terrestria?"

The nobleman nodded.

The sixth shining warrior flew above the great river and

poured a bluish gray liquid upon the waters. As Josiah watched in astonishment, the waters shriveled and then disappeared entirely. Within minutes, all that remained was a dry riverbed. "Preparations for the greatest battle in the Great War are being made," Sir Wisdom told Josiah. "The highway for the Kings of the East has just been prepared."

He looked up as a seventh shining warrior flew by. "The final vial of judgment is about to be emptied, and then will come a battle such as Terrestria has never seen." As the mighty warrior poured a clear liquid into the air, a great voice sounded across the skies, saying, "It is done."

Suddenly the air was filled with great voices and lightning and thunder. The mountain upon which Josiah and Sir Wisdom were standing began to tremble and shake. A nearby boulder split open with a loud report. Josiah grabbed his companion. "Sir Wisdom, what shall we do?"

"We are in no danger," the nobleman replied calmly. "But behold!"

With a loud, angry rumbling, the Great City at the base of the mountain began to shake as if in the grip of a ferocious animal. The buildings rocked and swayed. Dust rose high into the air. With a mighty explosion that shook the mountain, the Great City suddenly split into three parts. Building after building crumbled to the ground in piles of rubble.

The mountain upon which the two were standing trembled violently. Josiah cried out in fear. "Sir Wisdom! We're sinking!"

Even as he spoke, the mountain peak seemed to melt away beneath them and they sank faster and faster until they were standing upon a plain at the edge of the city. Josiah turned. The mountain was gone.

The plain suddenly grew dark and Josiah looked up to see

that dark, ominous clouds had blotted out the sun. As he watched, the clouds grew darker and darker, swelling and surging and boiling as they dropped lower and lower. The entire sky had a sinister, frightening appearance. An angry wind shrieked and howled, throwing dust and debris into the air like a spiteful child.

With a screaming, whistling noise, a large object fell from the skies to land with a loud crash upon the roof of a nearby building. Seconds later, another fell, and then another. Within moments, the skies were filled with the falling objects. The noise of their falling and the resulting crashes created an overwhelming barrage of sound.

"What are they?" Josiah cried aloud.

"Hailstones," Sir Wisdom replied. "Hailstones so large that they weigh more than eight stone apiece."

A myriad of screams and cries from within the Great City indicated that the enormous hailstones were having disastrous effects. The hailstones fell faster and faster until they became a torrent. Large trees snapped under the onslaught of falling ice; countless buildings were damaged or destroyed. Those peasants struck by hailstones were killed instantly.

"Such devastation," Josiah said quietly, as he surveyed the damage. "This was perhaps the worst plague of all." He was thoughtful for several minutes as he pondered the various plagues and the destruction that he had seen. "It will be horrendous to be left behind when King Emmanuel comes for his children, won't it?"

Sir Wisdom nodded. "The times of judgment will be the worst period in Terrestria's history. You do not want to be here when the judgments fall."

Hearing the sound of distant trumpets, Josiah turned. A large army was marching toward the Great City, using the dry riverbed as a highway. More than a thousand abreast, the columns of marching warriors stretched for miles. The sound of their marching feet reverberated like distant thunder in the mountains. Banners and standards flying above their close ranks displayed various coats of arms. "The armies of the Kings of the East," Sir Wisdom said.

Josiah was in awe as he watched the vast hordes of marching warriors. Rank upon rank, the armies swept into a huge natural basin that stretched for miles. Reaching the basin, they stood in tight formation. "Look how many there are!" Josiah said breathlessly. "There must be tens of thousands."

"Millions," Sir Wisdom replied.

The rhythmic sound of countless hoof beats drew his attention to the rear of the advancing army, and he saw huge divisions of mounted knights in dark armor. Powerful warhorses of every size and description trotted smartly in well-ordered ranks. Standards flying proudly from lances bore various coat of arms; most prominent were those bearing the red dragon. An uneasy feeling of impending doom swept over Josiah as he viewed the vast cavalry division.

"Did you ever see such horses?" Josiah breathed, partly in admiration, partly in fear.

"The Kings of the East have always been known for their magnificent horses," the nobleman replied.

The young prince turned. "Look to the north!" he exclaimed. "Here comes another huge army!"

As they watched, another vast horde swept in from the north and marched into the basin. The air was filled with the sounds of battle preparations—the sounds of marching feet, the clank of armor, and the rattling of weapons. With perfect precision the newcomers filed into place and took positions beside the armies of the Kings of the East. Swords, spears, and battleaxes were held aloft as they cried as one, "For Argamor! For Alphaomega! For Terrestria!" The valley shook with their cries. Moments later, tens of thousands of mounted warriors rode into the basin behind them.

The sound of millions of voices raised in cadence drew Josiah's attention to the west, and he turned to see additional armies flowing into the basin like an endless tide of humanity. Wave after wave of armored knights marched in tight ranks, stepping smartly in perfect synchronization, calling cadence as they marched. At the same time, another huge army marched in from the south, followed by large divisions of cavalry mounted on magnificent warhorses.

"Whose armies are these?" Josiah cried in astonishment. "Why are they assembling here?"

"These are the armies of all Terrestria," Sir Wisdom replied. "They have been called by Argamor and Alphaomega to fight against King Emmanuel for possession of Terrestria. This one great battle will stand forever as the greatest battle in the Great War, the greatest battle in history."

"Will Emmanuel..." Josiah hesitated.

"Will he what, my prince?"

"There are so many warriors—there must be millions!" Josiah blurted. "They have tens of thousands of magnificent warhorses. And look—they're bringing catapults and trebuchets, and...and dragons! Look, Sir Wisdom! They have dragons!" He looked at the nobleman with concern upon his countenance. "Will King Emmanuel be able to defeat all these? There are so many, and the war machines are so enormous!"

Sir Wisdom shook his head. "Josiah, Josiah. You have seen the mighty hand of Emmanuel, and yet still you doubt his power. My prince, His Majesty could defeat ten thousand armies of this size with just one word!"

Before long, the assembled armies completely filled the basin; the troops numbered in the countless millions. Dark warriors and Terrestrians alike stood at attention, eyes turned toward the dark, angry skies as if awaiting a challenge from the clouds. Evil and hatred emanated from their ranks like the stench of rotting flesh. Tension filled the air.

One division of dark knights began rattling their swords in their scabbards, and the action spread across the evil throng like wildfire. Millions of swords, spears, and battleaxes rattled menacingly or clashed against each other. Impatient, the warriors began stamping their feet in unison. The resulting cacophony was louder than a thousand thunderstorms.

Powerful warhorses began to prance impatiently. Others reared high in the air and snorted loudly to show their eagerness to engage in battle. A few whinnied anxiously, nervous in the presence of so much tension and excitement.

Three dark warlords mounted on three powerful black warhorses rode slowly, majestically, across the vast battleground. The assembled armies parted to let them pass. The warlords rode to the center of the valley and then reined to a stop. As one, they raised their swords high in the air. The sound of millions of cheering voices filled the air.

"Argamor, Alphaomega, and the False Prophet," Josiah whispered in dread as he watched the sinister trio. The shouts of accolade increased until the young prince closed his eyes in pain.

Suddenly, a hush fell across the vast armies of evil. The assembled throngs of dark warriors and evil Terrestrians fell silent; their weapons stood motionless. The horses quieted as though soothed by the touch of a capable stableman. The wind ceased its howling. Time seemed to stand still.

At that moment, the dark clouds above the battlefield parted in the middle and rolled to the sides of the horizon as though someone had opened the draperies at an enormous window. A golden beam of brilliant sunlight fell upon the assembled warriors; the dazzling rays reflected from polished armor with a blinding brilliance.

Murmurs of fear rippled across the ranks of the dark armies, for descending from the skies was an enormous white warhorse, broad in chest and powerful in limb, and upon his back was a warrior who would strike terror into the hearts of even the bravest. His eyes were as flames of fire and upon his head was a glittering golden crown. He was clothed in a vesture dipped in blood; and upon his vesture and upon his thigh was a name written: KING OF KINGS AND LORD OF LORDS.

"King Emmanuel," Josiah breathed.

Following King Emmanuel upon white warhorses of their own was a vast army of warriors dressed in white tunics and glistening white armor. Numbering in the millions, they rode from the clouds after their King, rank upon rank until the entire sky was filled with them.

"This will be a battle like no other," Sir Wisdom said quietly. "You are about to witness the wrath and power of the King of kings!"

Chapter Fifteen

As Prince Josiah watched in astonishment, an enormous shining warrior hovered above the silent battlefield. His form was huge; he blotted out the sun. "Come to me," he cried in a voice that rumbled like thunder. "Come to me, fowls of the air, and gather yourselves to the supper of the great King. He will feed you the flesh of kings, of captains, of mighty men, and of horses."

Even as he spoke, scavenger birds and birds of prey began to gather, circling the battlefield at great heights. Cormorants and eagles and falcons and vultures—together they numbered in the hundreds of thousands as they soared in never ending circles on motionless wings. Watching them, Josiah felt an icy chill go up his back.

King Emmanuel and his armies rode forward, downward, advancing toward the vast hordes of evil waiting for them on the ground. Somewhere in the skies, a shining warrior blew a mighty blast on a golden trumpet. Josiah held his breath.

Argamor rode forward, raising an enormous glittering sword. "Sons of Terrestria," he called in a mighty voice, "this is your chance to end the tyranny of Emmanuel once and for all! Today we shall seize the throne that is rightfully ours! Together we shall—"

Two screams of terror interrupted his speech and Josiah turned to see Alphaomega and the False Prophet suspended high in the air, struggling as if caught in the folds of a great invisible net.

"Take them," King Emmanuel commanded two of his shining warriors, who hovered nearby. "Bind them and cast them into the Furnace of Eternal Fire."

The two shining ones swooped down and bound the two captives as their Lord had commanded. As the shining warriors flew away carrying the False King and the False Prophet, their two captives shrieked with terror.

"Charge!" roared Argamor, brandishing his great sword and spurring his powerful warhorse forward. "Sons of Terrestria, this battle is for the kingdom!"

The armies of the Kings of the East surged forward, eager to join the battle, but the remaining armies stood still, rendered immobile by fear. One entire cavalry division in the northern army wheeled their mounts around and attempted to flee the battlefield. Here and there, individual dark warriors and Terrestrians threw down their weapons and turned to flee.

A trumpet sounded just then, loud and clear and strong, and the golden notes resounded triumphantly across the skies, echoing and re-echoing across the valley until it seemed that all of Terrestria rang with the sound. Millions of dark warriors and Terrestrians, trembling with terror, fell to their knees or tumbled forward to fall on their faces. Horses dropped as if dead.

"Charge!" Argamor roared again, his face livid with anger. "Sons of Terrestria, don't fail me now! This is your moment— this is your one great opportunity! Emmanuel cannot stand before us; we outnumber his forces three to one. Stand like the warriors you are and we shall defeat this tyrant once and for all!"

Even as Argamor spoke, a sharp sword issued from the mouth of King Emmanuel and began to smite the King's enemies with terrible swiftness. Thousands fell with each pass of the formidable blade. Within moments, the armies of Terrestria lay dead upon the vast battlefield.

With a cry of anguish, Argamor leaped from his horse and fell to his face before the King of kings. Laying his great sword in the dust, he cried, "My Lord, Emmanuel! The kingdom is yours, my Lord, yours forever! Spare me, my Lord, I beg you!"

King Emmanuel made a tiny gesture with his right hand. A mighty shining warrior dropped from the skies with a golden key in one hand and an enormous iron chain in the other. Placing the golden key in his belt, he reached down with one hand and seized Argamor by his beard. He pulled the evil warlord to his feet, bound him swiftly with the great chain, and dropped him face down in the dust. He placed his foot upon Argamor's neck and then looked to King Emmanuel for further orders.

For a moment, Josiah was speechless as he watched the spectacle. At last, he found his voice. "One warrior!" he exclaimed with delight. "It only took one shining warrior to bind Argamor!"

"Cast this evil beast into the bottomless abyss," King Emmanuel commanded the shining warrior. "He must be held captive for a thousand years, that he deceive the nations no more. Seal the abyss with my royal seal."

The scavenger birds swooped in and began to feed.

Prince Josiah turned and looked at Sir Wisdom, and without a word closed the book. Trembling, he dropped to his knees in the middle of the polished marble floor of the Library of Learning.

"It happened so quickly," the prince said, blinking back tears. "In moments, millions of them lay dead upon the battlefield."

"Such is the power of His Majesty," Sir Wisdom said quietly.

"But there were so many." Josiah looked questioningly at the nobleman. "What happened to them? To their souls, I mean."

"You do realize that what we have just seen is still in the future, do you not?"

Josiah nodded.

"This great battle has not yet taken place. But when it does, the souls of those slain in that battle will be sent to the Furnace of Eternal Fire. Forever."

"Is there no hope for them?" Josiah asked.

"Right now there is hope for any Terrestrian who will turn to Emmanuel, receive his pardon, and embrace him as Lord," Sir Wisdom told him, "but once death comes, it is forever too late."

After some time, when Josiah had recovered somewhat from the trauma of watching the great battle, Sir Wisdom told him, "There is yet another great event that you must witness before we leave the Library of Learning."

"I'm not sure that I can bear to see any more," Josiah replied with a sigh. "Though I must say that my heart thrilled at the appearance of my King. When I saw him, I found myself longing to be with him."

"This is one event that you will enjoy watching," the nobleman promised. "I want you to witness the reign of His Majesty over Terrestria. You may not realize it, but the judgments and events that we have just witnessed will cover a period of seven years."

"Seven years?" Josiah echoed.

His companion nodded. "Viewing the judgments in quick succession as we did, it may have seemed a much shorter period than that, since the book showed us just the highlights. But as I said, the period of Terrestrian future that we just visited will take seven years to unfold. Alphaomega will actually be in power for forty-two months, or three-and-a-half years."

He held out his hand. "May I see your book?"

Josiah handed it to him and he opened to a particular passage. "Now I want you to see the most glorious period in Terrestria's future: the thousand-year Terrestrian kingdom of Emmanuel. For one thousand glorious years, His Majesty will personally reign from the City of Zion. Perfect peace will be the order of the day, and righteousness and justice will prevail. Aye, the kingdom years will be glorious!" He handed the book back to Josiah.

Josiah's heart pounded with anticipation. "Will we see King Emmanuel again?"

Sir Wisdom nodded. "Aye, we will."

"Then let us go at once." Josiah stepped into the Book of the Apocalypse.

He and Sir Wisdom found themselves walking down a dusty country lane. The afternoon sun was warm and a pleasant breeze stirred in the treetops. Josiah spotted a rosebush growing beside the road and hurried over to it. "Look, Sir Wisdom," he called, "a rosebush growing in the wild." His eyes grew wide. "Look, sire, at the size of these roses! They are enormous, and each one is absolutely perfect!" He stared at the rosebush in utter amazement for a moment and then turned to his companion. "Sire, never have I seen wild roses such as these. They are by far the biggest roses I have ever seen, and not one of them has a blemish of any kind! Who could grow roses such as these?"

"They are growing wild, so they belong to no one," the nobleman answered. "Pick one."

Josiah reached out to pick a rose, grasping the stem carefully to avoid the thorns, and then a look of utter astonishment swept across his face. "Sire, there are no thorns! Whoever saw a rose with no thorns?"

"The curse has been removed from Terrestria," Sir Wisdom told him. "You will find that many things are different now."

The bleating of sheep drew their attention and they both turned to see a small boy leading a small flock down a small hill directly toward them. Josiah inhaled sharply and drew his sword. Just a pace or two behind the shepherd boy stalked a huge lion! Josiah raised his sword and called a warning to the boy. "Beware, lad—a lion is upon you!"

Sir Wisdom grabbed his arm. "He cannot hear you or see you. Just watch."

The young shepherd stepped down into the roadway and then paused as his flock gathered around him. To Josiah's astonishment, the lion stood beside the boy and the boy wrapped one arm around the huge beast's furry mane! Josiah turned and looked at Sir Wisdom for an explanation.

"As I said, the curse has been removed. Under the peaceful reign of King Emmanuel, even the wild animals are no longer wild. This lion poses no more threat to the lad or his sheep than would a newborn kitten."

Josiah was speechless.

He and Sir Wisdom followed the young shepherd and his flock to a humble dwelling nestled in the foothills of a range of majestic purple mountains. Wildflowers grew in profusion and the blossoms were bigger and brighter than any that Josiah had ever seen. The air was scented with their sweet perfume.

Butterflies danced in the sunshine while an array of brilliant hummingbirds darted from flower to flower. Songbirds in the trees filled the afternoon with their sweet melodies.

Josiah stopped and listened. "Sir Wisdom!"

"What is it, my prince?"

"Listen to the songbirds, sire! I cannot understand everything that they are singing, but their song includes the name of Emmanuel! I just heard it!"

"Why does that amaze you?" the old man asked, with a twinkle in his eye. "The creatures were made for Emmanuel's glory. Should not their songs praise his name?"

"This place is paradise," Josiah breathed.

"Terrestria is indeed paradise under the rule of Emmanuel," Sir Wisdom replied. "Argamor is imprisoned in the bottomless abyss, and so war and violence are but memories of the past. The curse has been removed, and now the ground produces food and beauty as never before. Apparently, King Emmanuel and his Father intend to show all of Terrestria just what their creation would have been had there been no rebellion."

"Daniel is home," a man's voice called, "but it looks like he brought home more than just the sheep."

A slender woman with a peaceful countenance stepped out of the house, followed by a young girl. Their eyes grew wide at the sight of the lion. "Daniel! Wherever did you get that?"

"May I keep him, Mother? May I?"

The young mother sighed. "Son, where did you find him?"

"He came out of the forest and found us, Mother. He just came over to us and lay down with the lambs. May I keep him? Please?"

"Daniel, he's enormous. Do you know how much an animal his size would eat? We couldn't afford to keep him."

"Are you forgetting, my good woman," a man's voice said, "that this beast will eat straw, rather than meat?" With these words, a tall young farmer stepped around the corner of the house.

The woman ran to her husband and put her arms around his waist. "Isaiah, he can't keep every animal he finds. Yesterday it was a bear; the day before that, it was a wolf! If we let Daniel keep every wild creature he finds, before long there won't be room for the people."

Her husband laughed. "Aye, but you didn't let him keep the bear, remember? I say we let him keep the lion. I'll help him gather grass and straw for it."

The woman smiled and shrugged. "Well, Daniel, you heard your father." She gave the boy a stern look. "But I won't have you bringing that beast into the house unless you have a suitable name for him! Do you hear me, young man?"

Daniel paused and then realized that his mother was teasing him. His face lit up with a delighted grin. "Oh, thank you, Father! Thank you, Mother!"

His mother smiled and hugged him. "Better get the sheep into their fold. Even with the creatures being what they are now, those sheep of yours seem to find a way to get lost without even trying!"

Sir Wisdom nudged Josiah. "How old do you think this farmer is?"

Josiah shrugged and studied the man for a moment. "Thirty-six? Thirty-eight?"

"I'll give you a hint," the nobleman said, with a trace of a smile. "The little girl, Deborah, is his great, great, great grand-daughter. Daniel is her great, great, great uncle."

Josiah stared at him. "Surely you jest, sire."

Sir Wisdom shook his head. "I'm very serious."

"I won't even try to guess the farmer's age."

"Isaiah, the farmer, is one hundred seventy-six years old."

Josiah studied the nobleman's face for a moment, decided that he wasn't jesting, and then studied the farmer with awe. "That is incredible, sire!"

"As I mentioned, when His Majesty establishes his thousand-year kingdom, the curse will be removed from Terrestria. People will live to a great age."

"The thousand-year reign of King Emmanuel sounds magnificent, Sir Wisdom!" Josiah blurted eagerly. "It almost sounds as wonderful as living in the Golden City of the Redeemed!"

"You and I cannot even begin to imagine just how fantastic his kingdom will be," the nobleman replied. "His Majesty has delights planned for his children of which they cannot even dream. Emmanuel's kingdom is definitely something to look forward to."

"I can't wait!" The young prince turned about, slowly drinking in the splendor of the beauty around him. Abruptly, he turned to Sir Wisdom. "Where is King Emmanuel? We haven't seen him yet."

"Emmanuel reigns from the City of Zion. Would you like to see him?"

"Aye, I would like that very much."

"Then lighten your feet and we will go there. It is too far to walk."

"Lighten my feet? What do you mean, sire?"

"Lighten your feet," the nobleman repeated, with a twinkle in his eyes. "Like this!" To Josiah's utter amazement, the old man floated a few feet above the roadway for a moment or two and then dropped back to stand upon his feet.

Josiah was astounded. "Sire, I have seen some incredible things today, but this is the most amazing of all! How did you do it?"

"When His Majesty comes and takes his children to the

Golden City," Josiah's companion explained, "he will give them perfect bodies in the image and likeness of his own glorious body. Those new glorified bodies will feel no pain, experience no sickness, injury, or disease, and will be forever free from the threat of death. Since they will be perfect, they will not be under the constraints that your present mortal body is."

"Constraints?" Josiah was confused.

"Constraints such as gravity," Sir Wisdom replied with a grin, as he floated in the air once again. "Come on, my prince, give it a try. You'll find that it's quite an incredible experience."

Josiah's heart pounded with anticipation. "How do I do it, sire?"

"Simply lift both feet at the same time. I think you'll find that traveling in this manner is quite a delight."

The young prince timidly lifted both feet and found himself floating ten or twelve feet above the narrow country lane. "Sir Wisdom! This is incredible!" His mind raced. "What else will our new bodies do?"

"You wouldn't believe me if I told you," the nobleman replied with a grin. "Come on, let's fly to the City of Zion and see King Emmanuel."

Chapter Sixteen

The countryside far below was a peaceful vista of verdant forests, sapphire blue lakes and rivers, golden brown fields, and glistening white cities and villages. From the air, Terrestria looked much like a magnificent patchwork quilt.

Josiah laughed in delight as he watched a coach make its way along a country road. "This is the way to travel!" he cried, dropping into a dive like a falcon and then soaring back up above the clouds. "How high are we, Sir Wisdom?"

"We're soaring with the eagles, lad," the nobleman answered. "Look!"

Josiah turned and saw that there was indeed a golden eagle less than a hundred yards to his right. "Will we really fly like this when King Emmanuel takes us home to the Golden City?"

"What does your book say, Josiah? 'We know that, when he shall appear, we shall be like him; for we shall see him as he is.' After Emmanuel died for you and came back to life, his resurrected body could fly, so yours will too."

"I can't wait for that!" Josiah responded. "This is just a bit frightening at first, but it is so exhilarating! Once Emmanuel comes for us and we go to the Golden City, life is going to be quite exciting, isn't it?"

"You don't know the half of it. His Majesty has so many delights planned for you, your life is going to be one thrilling adventure after another. Aye, life in the Golden City of the Redeemed will be incredibly fulfilling, and your life during the thousand-year reign of Emmanuel will be just as thrilling."

Sir Wisdom pointed downward. "The City of Zion is just ahead. Let's begin our descent."

As the pair approached the magnificent main gate of the beautiful City of Zion, they soared less than two hundred feet above the roadway. Spotting two young men on horseback, Josiah dropped lower for a closer look. To his astonishment, he saw that the older of the two riders was his brother-in-law, Selwyn! His companion was a sturdy-looking young man with curly hair and a friendly smile. Knowing that the riders could neither see nor hear him, Josiah flew back up to catch up with the nobleman, who by now was flying over the city.

"Did you see the two riders?" he called. "One of them was Selwyn!"

"Did you not recognize the other rider?" Sir Wisdom asked as Josiah came alongside.

Josiah shook his head. "He was quite a bit younger than Selwyn, but I have no idea who he was."

Sir Wisdom gave him a strange look. "The second rider was your son, Ethan."

"Ethan?" Josiah wheeled about in midair to drop down for another look, but the two riders had entered the city and were not in sight. Disappointed, he hurried to rejoin Sir Wisdom.

Just ahead was a magnificent park area with luscious green lawns, lovely flower gardens, pleasant shade trees, and a crystal-clear stream meandering lazily across it. Here and there, happy people strolled along on footpaths that wound their way through the park, crossing the stream on delightful little arched bridges. The air was filled with the delicious fragrance of wildflowers and the cheerful choruses of songbirds. The atmosphere in the beautiful park was one of peace and contentment.

"I think we'll find King Emmanuel here," Sir Wisdom said, dropping toward the park. Josiah followed.

"I just noticed that there are no castles," Josiah remarked, as he and the nobleman alighted on the path and began to walk through the park. "Why are there no castles?"

"The castles were built for protection from the enemy. With Argamor imprisoned in the bottomless abyss, there is no need for castles."

A group of hundreds of children made their way toward the two visitors, laughing and chattering happily as they walked. Their faces were alive with joy and contentment; never before had Josiah seen anyone so happy. And then Josiah saw King Emmanuel. The children were surrounding him, holding his hands and talking with him as they strolled along, laughing and enjoying being in his presence.

Josiah stood still as the joyous group passed him. He watched Emmanuel's face, thrilling at the gentle love he saw in the King's eyes as he talked with the children. His heart stirred with longing. Oh, that Emmanuel would come soon and take him to the Golden City of the Redeemed that he might actually be in the King's presence!

Sir Wisdom touched him on the shoulder. "It will be soon, my prince, very soon," he said softly, and Josiah realized that the old man knew exactly what he was thinking.

"The children are so happy, sire, so very happy! What a wondrous thing it is to watch King Emmanuel with the children!"

"He walks with them here in the park each and every

afternoon," Sir Wisdom told him. "The children love it."

Josiah watched wistfully as the noisy, happy group sauntered down the path. His heart stirred with love as he watched his gracious King, and the deep longing returned. "How long, Sir Wisdom," he asked, "how long until His Majesty returns and takes us to the Golden City?"

"It won't be long now," came the reply. "Not long at all."

"Thank you for bringing me here," the young prince said thoughtfully. "Today I have seen enough of Emmanuel's thousand-year kingdom to know that it will be absolutely glorious! I have always looked forward to living with His Majesty in the Golden City, but I have never given much thought to his reign here upon Terrestria. Now, I can't wait!"

The nobleman smiled. "It will be glorious indeed. Shall we return to the Library of Learning? There is so much more that I could show you, but your mind would not be able to hold it all. Suffice it to say that your King has planned such a magnificent future for his children and has so many delights in store that you will be thrilled with every moment of it!"

Josiah closed his book. "You have mentioned several times that Emmanuel's kingdom will last for a thousand years," Josiah said, as he and Sir Wisdom stood once again before the Apocalypse painting. "What will happen after the thousand years?"

Sir Wisdom turned toward the painting and Josiah could see that he was wrestling with a decision. "I could show you by visiting in the book again," he said slowly, "but perhaps it would be faster if I simply told you."

Together they strolled across the vast library. "I told you that Argamor will be imprisoned in the bottomless abyss during the thousand years of Emmanuel's Terrestrian kingdom. At the end of the thousand years, for some reason, Emmanuel will loose Argamor for a little season. Argamor will go out and once again deceive the nations and then gather them together again to fight against King Emmanuel one last time."

"Why would he even try?" Josiah asked with a snort. "Would he not know that he has no chance of winning?"

"Argamor has lost battle after battle in the Great War," replied the nobleman, "and yet he keeps trying."

"What will happen in that last battle?"

"This, of course, will be the last battle ever," Sir Wisdom told him. "The nations that follow Argamor will come together against the City of Zion. Emmanuel will simply send fire down from the skies and destroy them all. Argamor will then be thrown into the Furnace of Eternal Fire to be tormented forever."

"I will rejoice when that happens," Josiah said fervently.

"As will we all," Sir Wisdom replied. "But then follows the saddest event in all of Terrestrian history."

"What is that?"

"The trial of the ages will take place," the old man replied soberly. "Every person who has ever walked upon Terrestrian soil will stand before Emmanuel to be judged. At that trial, anyone whose name is not written in the Book of the Redeemed will—"

"I witnessed that judgment," Josiah interrupted, as a memory stirred in his mind. "I was on my quest for the seven castles when I visited the Castle of Knowledge. At that judgment, King Emmanuel was seated on an enormous white throne, and a great shining attendant checked the Book of the Redeemed for each person's name. Anyone whose name was not written in the book was sentenced to the Furnace of Eternal Fire to be tormented forever."

He sighed. "It was the most heart-rending event that I have ever witnessed."

Together the prince and the nobleman passed from the great library into a tiny courtyard alive with flowering trees and colorful flower gardens. A small spring bubbled up in the center of the courtyard; the crystal-clear water flowed along a rock-lined channel and disappeared beneath the wall at the opposite end.

"After that great judgment day," Sir Wisdom said, "the Golden City will be totally rebuilt, and His Majesty will also create a new Terrestria. Emmanuel's children will live with him forever in the Golden City of the Redeemed, with instant access to every part of Terrestria. What a magnificent future you have as the son of King Emmanuel!"

The old man took a seat on a stone bench in the courtyard, so Josiah sat beside him. "Do you know why I brought you here, my prince? Do you know why it was so important to see what Emmanuel has planned for his children?"

"I have learned much, sire," Josiah replied. "I have learned much about His Majesty's plans for his children, but I have learned more about the King himself. To be honest, I had no idea that Emmanuel was so powerful! When I saw how easily he conquered the armies of Terrestria, and how easily he defeated Argamor, I realized that there are no limits to his power."

"And that is exactly what I wanted you to see," Sir Wisdom said quietly. "I know that you have been discouraged lately, especially after losing Ethan and seemingly losing Gilda, and I know that there have been times when you have wondered if Argamor will win the Great War and seize control of Terrestria. Earlier you spoke of wanting to lay down your sword and stop being a knight in Emmanuel's service. I thought you ought to see that you are on the winning side."

"I have been encouraged by what I have seen," Josiah replied eagerly, "and I thank you for enabling me to see it. But what am I to do for Gilda? Sire, I do not even know where she is! I had thought that she was the prisoner of Lady Acrimonious in the bramble-covered castle, but it seems that I was wrong. I could not find her there."

"Let's return to the Castle of Faith," said the nobleman. "The bramble-covered castle that you describe is none other than the Castle of Bitterness. Gilda is fighting her own Great War, a war that now rages within her soul. Perhaps I can help you with a plan to rescue her."

Chapter Seventeen

Prince Josiah and Prince Selwyn rode carefully along a narrow forest trail. "I hate to even think of going into the Valley of Discouragement," Josiah called to Selwyn, who was in the lead. "I traveled through the Valley of Discouragement once on my quest for the seven castles. It was the most dreadful place that I have ever encountered—I thought that I would never get out."

"I also dread that dark valley," Selwyn replied, "but Sir Wisdom told us that the valley is where we will find the Ring of Empathy that we must use to rescue Gilda."

The forest trail crested a small rise and Selwyn reined to a halt. "Look, Josiah! The enemy camp is now enormous! Look how many warriors there are!"

"There must be thousands," Josiah said softly, as he surveyed the wide valley below. "Hundreds of thousands!"

The enemy camp now extended for miles. An endless city of tents lay before them, thousands upon thousands, each flying the black standard bearing Argamor's coat of arms, the red dragon. A score of enormous catapults and at least a dozen trebuchets stood in the center of the camp, looming over the tents like gigantic mechanical warriors.

The camp was a beehive of activity. At the closest edge of the camp, open forges glowed red-hot, and the constant ringing of hammers against anvils told the two princes that a number of blacksmiths were busy at work. "They're making weapons of war," Josiah told Selwyn.

Another crew of workmen was assembling several tall wooden towers, which both men knew were siege towers used for attacking castles. "Why are they building them here?" Selwyn asked. "They can't move them through the forest."

"They'll disassemble them here and reassemble them at the battle site," Josiah replied.

Selwyn pointed. "Look. Workers are capping the ends of those huge logs with iron. What are those for?"

"Battering rams!" Josiah answered. "They're making those to assault the gates of the castles!"

"They've got more than a score of battering rams," Selwyn remarked. "Why would they need that many?" His eyes grew wide as he turned to Josiah. "They're planning to attack a number of castles, Josiah! If they have a score of battering rams and they're still making more, it looks as if Argamor and his dark knights are planning to attack every castle in Terrestria!"

"If that is what they are planning, then King Emmanuel is coming for his children very, very soon."

Even as Josiah and Selwyn watched, additional companies of dark warriors marched into the valley. "Let's leave this vile place," Selwyn suggested. "You can sense the evil and the hatred for Emmanuel emanating from this valley. It's like the stench of rotting garbage."

"Aye," Josiah agreed. "And we need to hurry to the Valley of Discouragement and obtain the Ring of Empathy, then go to the Castle of Bitterness in order to rescue Gilda. As soon as we have skirted this valley and are on the other side, let's stop and send petitions to His Majesty asking for his help in this dangerous quest."

After a ride of nearly two hours, the two princes approached a gloomy valley that ran for miles in both directions. "The Valley of Discouragement," Josiah said uneasily, as he and Selwyn dismounted and tied their horses to nearby trees. "I dread this place."

"This won't take long," Selwyn replied. "We'll be in and out before you know it." He tied a rope to a stout tree and threw the end down into the canyon. Sliding carefully down the rope, Josiah and Selwyn lowered themselves easily into the Valley of Discouragement.

Josiah stood in the center of the valley and looked around with a growing sense of dismay. An unusual twilight seemed to hang over the Valley of Discouragement like a translucent shroud; the mountainside above the valley was brightly lit and he could see it clearly, but somehow, the valley was dark and filled with grotesque shadows. It was as if the light of the sun simply could not penetrate the gloom of the valley.

Selwyn gripped his arm. "Let's get the ring and get out of this place."

Josiah nodded nervously. His heart raced and his chest constricted with fear. He felt as if he could not breathe.

"Josiah! Are you all right?"

Josiah shook his head and struggled to breathe. "I—I'm afraid of this place, Selwyn. Once when I fell into this valley, it was so very hard to get back out."

"You know now how to get back out, though," Selwyn told

him. "And I'm here with you so that we can be a source of strength for each other."

"I—I need to send a petition," Josiah faltered. Opening his book, he withdrew the parchment and quickly sent an urgent petition to the Golden City. At once, a warm peace flooded his soul. He looked at Selwyn. "Now I am ready."

Selwyn looked around. "Where do you suppose that we will find the Ring of Empathy? This valley is so long; it could be anywhere."

"Sir Wisdom said to look where the shadows are the darkest," Josiah replied. "Come on."

Staying close together for the reassuring presence of each other's company, the two princes slowly traversed the dark valley, carefully searching each shadowy nook and crevice. The gloom and darkness of the place weighed on them like millstones upon their shoulders, oppressive and nearly overwhelming. After searching the shadows and gloom for more than a mile, Josiah pointed to a dark depression in the canyon wall. "There! That cavern. That's the darkest place yet."

As they approached the cavern, fear swept over the two princes, paralyzing in its intensity. Josiah began to tremble. Selwyn noticed. "Josiah, what's wrong?"

"The V-Valley of D-Death," Josiah stammered. "Selwyn, this is the Valley of Death! It's as though Ethan has just died, and I feel the same great loss all over again! Selwyn, I can't bear this pain!"

"Yea, though I walk through the valley of the shadow of death, I will fear no evil, for thou art with me," Selwyn quoted. "Josiah, look to King Emmanuel for strength."

"Would you go into the cavern alone and look for the ring?" Josiah pleaded. "I...I cannot."

Selwyn nodded grimly and swallowed hard. "Stay here."

Opening his book to dispel the darkness of the cavern, he ventured in alone. The darkness seemed to swallow him up. Though he was just a few paces away, Josiah could not see him.

Josiah waited anxiously.

After what seemed like an eternity, Selwyn emerged from the darkness. His face was ashen and his hands trembled. "I-I didn't know how great was your loss when Ethan died," he said, struggling to fight back tears, "but now I think I understand." He hugged Josiah. "I now know what Gilda is feeling."

He smiled sadly and held up a glistening golden ring. "But I got what we came for."

Josiah was touched by Selwyn's willingness to venture into the dark cavern. "Thank you, my brother," he said fervently. He took the golden ring from Selwyn's outstretched hand and slipped it onto his own finger. At once, the ring began to glow. The young prince watched in amazement as the ring glowed brighter and brighter. "It's getting hot!" he yelped. "It's burning me."

"The ring grew hot when I slipped it on my finger," Selwyn replied. "I think perhaps it's enchanted."

"I can't keep it on much longer," Josiah moaned, wincing in pain. "It's getting hotter and hotter."

"Take it off," Selwyn urged.

Josiah snatched the ring off and tossed it back and forth from hand to hand. The glowing immediately began to subside. When the ring had cooled somewhat, Josiah held it between his thumb and forefinger and studied it curiously. "Why should the ring cause pain to the one who wears it?"

"It's the Ring of Empathy," Selwyn replied. "Perhaps you were feeling the pain of another."

Josiah glanced at him in surprise. "Gilda's pain?"

Selwyn nodded. "Perhaps."

Josiah was thoughtful as he pocketed the ring. "Perhaps even I do not understand the depth of Gilda's pain and loss. Perhaps this is why we must have the Ring of Empathy to rescue her."

He took a deep breath and looked around. "Now let's get out of this wretched valley."

"You know the way," Selwyn replied. "Sing praises."

Josiah turned toward the canyon wall. He took a deep breath and lifted his voice in song, "O that my tongue could somehow sing/Worthy praises to my King." A shaft of golden sunlight suddenly pierced the gloom of the Valley of Discouragement like a beacon of hope and promise; the golden rays lifted Josiah's spirits immediately.

"Emmanuel has ransomed me," Josiah sang. The sunlight grew brighter; a rainbow appeared above the valley. "Emmanuel has set me free." The darkness of the valley had been almost completely dispelled and Josiah could now see a golden path leading up to the upper rim of the valley. Looking back to make sure that Selwyn was following, he hurried toward it. Side by side, continuing to lift their voices in praise to their King, Josiah and Selwyn walked to the top of the golden trail. As they took the next step, they realized that they were now free of the Valley of Discouragement and they both shouted for joy. Breaking into song once more, they again praised the name of King Emmanuel, and the valley below them rang with the joyful sound of their voices.

"May we never have to enter this dread valley again," Selwyn said fervently, as he and Josiah took one last look.

"Well, if it isn't two of Emmanuel's knights," a taunting voice snarled, and the two princes spun around, startled, to see a dozen dark knights blocking the path with swords drawn. "We'll take that ring," the leader of the dark knights demanded. "Hand it over or die."

"We are on a quest that cannot wait," Josiah replied, snatching a parchment from his book and then swinging the book to transform it into the sword. "Stand aside and let us pass without hindrance."

"I asked for the ring, knave, and I will have it, even if it means your death. Now give it to me."

Prince Selwyn drew his sword.

"Stand aside, servant of Argamor," Josiah demanded boldly, "for we are the sons of His Majesty and we bear his invincible sword. We will not be delayed on our quest."

"Surrender the ring or die," the dark knight snarled.

"I'm not waiting for them to attack," Josiah said to Selwyn. "Let's attack first and put them on the defensive!"

Shouting the name of their King, the two princes leaped forward and engaged the dark knights in battle. Josiah swung his sword with all his might and inflicted a serious wound upon the leader of the dark knights. "You know, I'm glad to see opposition from Argamor's forces," he said to Selwyn, who fought with equal ardor beside him. "The fact that they are opposing us tells me that we are on the right path in this quest to rescue Gilda."

"Praise Emmanuel, it means that Argamor fears that we will be successful," Selwyn replied, dropping a dark knight with one blow from his sword.

A tall, broad-shouldered knight suddenly leaped at Selwyn, swinging a dreadful battleaxe with all his strength. Selwyn deflected the blow with his Shield of Faith, but the impact knocked him backwards and slightly off balance. The big knight charged straight at the young prince, striking Selwyn's Breastplate of Righteousness with his shoulder and knocking him heavily to the ground. The dark knight again raised the battleaxe.

"Josiah!"

Josiah was engaged in a desperate struggle with several enemy knights and knew that he could not reach Selwyn in time. Opening his left hand, he released a petition. Selwyn's attacker suddenly flew backwards through the air a distance of six or eight yards and landed on his back with a resounding crash of armor. Selwyn was on him in an instant and ended his life.

Moments later, all twelve dark knights lay dead upon the ground. The two young princes sent petitions of thanksgiving to King Emmanuel in response to the great victory. As they placed their books within their doublets, Selwyn turned to Josiah. "Thank you for the petition," he said gratefully. "You sent it just in time."

"I am learning to keep a petition ready at all times," Josiah replied quietly. "This is one of those times when it was urgently needed." He glanced at the motionless forms upon the ground. "Let's find the Castle of Bitterness and rescue Gilda."

Prince Josiah's heart pounded with anticipation as he and Selwyn approached the forbidding Castle of Bitterness hidden in the brambles. One part of him wanted to flee in terror while another part thrilled at the idea of finding Gilda. The wind howled like a tormented spirit, moaning and groaning in the trees and flinging bits of dirt and debris into the faces of the young princes as if it resented their presence. The skies were dark and the castle seemed to glow with an unearthly greenish light. Lightning slashed across the sky and thunder boomed angrily in reply. Fear gripped Josiah's heart.

He drew his sword as he stepped onto the decaying drawbridge, and Selwyn followed his example. Their footsteps on the rotting timbers sounded hollowly in the moat below, echoing and re-echoing with a strange rhythm that again made Josiah think of a beating heart. He and Selwyn paused long enough to send petitions to King Emmanuel.

Using their swords, they cleared most of the brambles from the portcullis and the main gate, half expecting that the tangled vegetation would grow back immediately. It did not. Transforming his sword into the book, Josiah opened the cover and removed a small golden key. He touched the key to the portcullis. With the groan of protesting pulleys and the rattle of heavy chains, the iron barrier slowly began to rise of its own accord.

Josiah and Selwyn hurried forward and ducked beneath the moving portcullis. Josiah touched the Key of Faith to the gate, which opened immediately with the protesting groan of rusty hinges.

The barbican was dark and gloomy, and Josiah's heart constricted with fear. Trembling, he swung the book to transform it into the sword. He and Selwyn passed through the main gate and into the barbican, moving slowly and cautiously and scanning each shadowy nook and cranny for any sign of opposition. But the barbican appeared to be empty, and the only sounds they heard were the wail of the wind in the towers and the pounding of their own hearts.

Josiah's thoughts turned to Gilda. *Will we find her here in the castle tower? Is she all right?*

The two princes passed through the inner gate and entered the bailey of the castle. Spotting the doorway on the far side of the bailey, Josiah pointed it out to Selwyn. "That's where we're going. See the opening in the brambles? That opens on the corridor that leads to the tower where we will find Gilda."

They hurried toward it. Josiah glanced behind them to make sure that they were not being followed, and then he and Selwyn stepped through a doorway into a musty, dimly lit corridor. Josiah held his sword against his side until it transformed into the book and then opened its pages to allow its light to illuminate the corridor.

To Josiah's great horror, the tall suit of armor was standing once again in its place with the tremendous broadsword in its hands. "Selwyn, beware!" Josiah hissed in a loud whisper. "That suit of armor will attack us, and believe me, it fights with a vengeance!" Fearfully, he swung the book to transform it into the sword.

Chapter Eighteen

Holding their swords ready, the two princes crept warily past the suit of armor, but the armor stood motionless. Once they had safely reached the end of the corridor, Selwyn turned to Josiah. "I thought you said it would fight us."

"It did last time."

Selwyn snorted. "And you say that *I* have a wild imagination."

Two minutes and several passages later, Josiah led Selwyn up a narrow, spiraling flight of stairs. "This leads to the tower where Gilda was held," Josiah said, "but the solar was empty when I reached it."

Taking his Key of Faith from the book, he unlocked the door at the top of the stairs and opened it. The two princes hurried into the solar. "It's empty, Josiah."

"As it was last time," Josiah replied with a sigh. "But I was certain that this was the tower! I saw Gilda from the balcony."

"Give me the Ring of Empathy," Selwyn requested. Josiah handed it to him.

Selwyn slipped the ring on his finger and held it close to the lock on the door. "Look, Josiah. The Ring of Empathy is barely glowing, and besides, your Key of Faith opened the door by itself. This is not the right tower, Josiah! The Ring of Empathy is intended to help open another door. Somewhere there is another tower in this castle. That has to be where Gilda is being held."

Josiah thought it through. "That makes sense," he admitted. "But where? I've searched this whole side of the castle and checked out every door that could possibly lead to a tower."

"Did you check the door in the corridor behind the suit of armor?"

Josiah was surprised. "There was a door behind the empty knight?"

"Sure! Didn't you see it? It was as though the suit of armor was guarding it."

"So that's why the empty knight attacked last time, but not this time," Josiah said thoughtfully. "Last time I was attempting to search the entire castle; this time I was heading straight for this tower."

"Which means that the armor will attack us when we attempt to pass through the door that it is guarding," Selwyn said ruefully.

Josiah laughed at the look on Selwyn's face. "Aye, I think you're right."

Selwyn shrugged. "Well, let's find out. At least there are two of us."

"That may not be enough."

Selwyn stared at him. "What do you mean?"

"This knight, or suit of armor, or whatever it is, fights with a ferocity that you will not believe. Its strength is incredible and its speed will catch you off guard. Not only that, it somehow seems to know what you are thinking and counters your moves almost before you make them."

Selwyn frowned. "Then how did you defeat it?"

Josiah shrugged. "I don't know. Just when I thought it was going to kill me, I saw a fiery streak of light and the armor seemed to explode." He paused. "You know what I think?"

"What?"

"It was almost as if one of Emmanuel's shining warriors came to my rescue and defeated that thing before it could kill me."

Selwyn was thoughtful. "It's possible. The book says that the shining ones are ministers, sent forth to minister for them who shall be heirs of salvation. That's us."

Together they hurried back down the spiraling stairs and passed back through the long corridor. Josiah drew his sword as they neared the door guarded by the empty suit of armor. Selwyn, who was a step ahead, abruptly stopped. "Oh, no!"

Josiah raised his sword. "What's wrong?"

"They are three of them!" Selwyn whispered. "Now we're in for a real battle!"

Josiah stood perfectly still as he waited for his eyes to adjust to the gloom of the corridor. Just as Selwyn had said, three enormous knights with huge broadswords stood guarding the secluded door. Emblazoned across each knight's breastplate was Argamor's coat of arms.

Josiah let out his breath in a long sigh. "If the second and third knights are the equal of the first in strength, speed, and fighting skills, we are in for a fierce battle," he said quietly. "Selwyn, we don't stand a chance! You cannot imagine the ferocity with which this thing fought! Imagine my surprise when I found out that the armor was empty; there was no knight inside." He glanced again at the three dark warriors. "I suppose they're all hollow, nothing but empty armor like the first."

Selwyn grinned. "So if we win, you're saying that it will be a hollow victory?"

Josiah groaned. "This is hardly the time for levity."

Selwyn shrugged. "Sorry."

Josiah raised his sword. "I'm going to move toward the door and see what happens. Be ready to come to my aid."

Selwyn nodded. "I'm with you. Be careful."

Trying his best to keep his sword from trembling, Josiah advanced cautiously toward the three dark knights. They stood motionless, broadswords raised, as though waiting. When Josiah was five or six paces from the door, one knight leaped forward, swinging his broadsword in a lightning quick motion that caught the young prince off guard. He barely got his shield up in time.

The ferocious blow struck Josiah's shield with a clanging sound that reverberated throughout the castle. The force of the strike sent Josiah tumbling backwards. His enormous adversary stepped back into position, raising his sword once again and standing motionless as if nothing had happened.

"Let me try," Selwyn said, as Josiah crept back and caught his breath. "For Emmanuel!" Raising his sword, Selwyn sprang toward the door. A different dark knight leaped forward, dealing the young prince a blow that lifted him off his feet and hurled him backwards three yards. Selwyn stood feebly to his feet. "It nearly split my Shield of Faith in two," he ruefully told Josiah.

Josiah was thoughtful. "It's as if they're guarding a well-defined zone," he told Selwyn. "As long as we don't cross a certain line, they do nothing. But once we step into that zone, they come to life. Watch." He crept toward the door.

"Josiah! Be careful!"

Josiah inched toward the three knights, watching them closely for any sign of movement. As he approached the spot where his actions had provoked the first assault, he slowed, creeping forward an inch at a time. As he slid his right foot forward half an inch, one of the knights started to raise his sword. Josiah immediately leaped back. Slowly, the sword dropped back into position.

"The one on the left is defending the door against you," Selwyn whispered, when Josiah had rejoined him. "The one on the right is after me. What is the one in the middle going to do?"

Josiah studied the three enormous adversaries. "I only see one way to overcome these dark knights, or whatever they are."

Selwyn frowned. "What is that?"

"You go against them," Josiah replied, "while I send petitions to Emmanuel." He transformed his sword, took out the parchment, and commenced to write.

Moments later, as he released the petition, Selwyn charged forward. Instantly, all three dark knights raised their broadswords and leaped forward to do battle with the young prince. "Josiah!" Selwyn cried in terror.

Three streaks of blinding light slashed across the darkness of the castle corridor. The three dark knights seemed to explode in front of Selwyn. Dark breastplates, greaves, vambraces, and gauntlets clattered down around him.

Selwyn lowered his sword and let out his breath. He glanced at the various pieces of armor scattered about the floor. "Aye, you were right. They're empty."

Josiah opened his book, took out a parchment, and quickly wrote a message to King Emmanuel:

> *"My Lord, King Emmanuel:*
> *We are grateful for the victory over the three dark adversaries.*
> *My Lord, we believe that we are very close to finding Gilda.*
> *Guide us, we humbly ask, and help us to rescue her from the*
> *Castle of Bitterness. Give us victory, and restore her to your*
> *service.*
>
> *Your son, Prince Josiah."*

Raising his hand, Josiah released the petition and watched as it shot through the stone wall of the dank castle on its way to the Golden City. His heart thrilled to know that Emmanuel had received his earnest plea.

The door in the corridor opened easily, and, as Josiah had anticipated, just beyond it were spiraling stairs that led upward. The two princes hurried to the top. Josiah inserted his Key of Faith into the lock and then struggled to turn it. He let out a sigh of frustration. "It doesn't work."

"Just as I thought," Selwyn said, staring at the door. "The Key of Faith and the Ring of Empathy will open it. It takes both."

Josiah slipped the ring onto his finger and then cried out in pain as the ring began to blaze with light. "It hurts, Selwyn! It hurts as never before!"

"Open the door," Selwyn urged. "Hurry! With the Ring of Empathy on your finger, you can open the door."

The ring was engulfed in flame. Josiah grimaced in agony. "I—I can't Selwyn! It hurts too much!" He sank to his knees, clawing desperately at the ring in an attempt to remove it.

"It's for Gilda!" Selwyn cried. "Open the door for Gilda!"

"For Gilda, and for King Emmanuel!" Josiah shouted, struggling to his feet as though burdened with an enormous weight. He lunged for the door, grabbed the key, and twisted it quickly. The door creaked open. Josiah snatched the Ring of Empathy from his finger and hurled it to the floor.

As the door opened, Selwyn sprang into the room with Josiah right on his heels. The small, circular solar was covered in dust, with cobwebs festooning the walls and an ancient spinning wheel. In the center of the room stood a sagging bed, and upon the bed sat Gilda, glassy-eyed and motionless. "Gilda," Josiah cried, overcome with emotion, "I've come to take you home!"

"Well, well, if it isn't the petitioning prince," a contemptuous voice purred, and Josiah spun around to see a tall warrior in dark armor with the familiar red dragon emblazoned across the breastplate. The warrior was slender, with long, raven-black hair, and Josiah realized that this was a woman. "Prince Josiah, what an honor to have your presence in the Castle of Bitterness!" The woman threw back her head and laughed, and Josiah couldn't miss the contempt in her voice. "My name is Mara."

"I have come to take Gilda home to the Castle of Faith," Josiah said evenly. "You are Lady Acrimonious, the Duchess of Discontent, and she has been your prisoner long enough!"

"You have it all wrong, my presumptuous prince," the woman said sweetly, though her eyes burned with hatred and contempt. "Gilda is my guest, not my prisoner." She fingered a small, glowing pendant hanging on a golden chain about her neck. "Gilda does not want to go with you."

"I do not want to go with you," Gilda repeated in a hollow voice.

Josiah stared at her in dismay. "Gilda, you must come with me! You're my wife!"

"She does not want to return to the Castle of Faith," the duchess said, again fingering the glowing purple pendant.

"I do not want to return to the Castle of Faith," Gilda repeated. Her eyes were wide and staring, but she looked at no one as she spoke.

"She no longer wants to serve Emmanuel," the duchess said with glee.

"I no longer want to serve Emmanuel."

"She never wants to see you again."

"I never want to see you again."

"Gilda!" Prince Josiah cried, "don't say such things! You don't know what you're saying—surely you don't mean such things!"

A long, glowing sword suddenly appeared in Lady Acrimonious' hand. "Vacate my castle, Prince Josiah, and take your friend with you, or you shall both forfeit your lives."

"I will not leave without my wife," Josiah replied.

The duchess' hand went to the pendant. "She does not love you any longer; why would you insist on staying?"

"I do not love you any longer; why would you insist on staying?" Gilda said the words without expression or movement, except for the motion of her lips.

Selwyn stepped close to Josiah. "She's controlling Gilda with the glowing purple pendant," he whispered.

"I just realized that," Josiah replied, "but how do we destroy the pendant, or get it away from her?"

"Distract her," Selwyn suggested. "I'll try to get the pendant from her." He stepped toward the bed as if to talk with Gilda.

"Stay away from her," the duchess ordered.

"She's my sister," Selwyn retorted. "I'll talk with her if I wish."

In an instant, the point of the glowing sword was pressed painfully against Selwyn's throat. "Step away from her, foolish prince, or your life ends right now."

Selwyn complied.

Unnoticed by the duchess, Josiah released a petition. He then stepped forward to confront her with his sword. "Drop the weapon, or I will run you through," he challenged. As the duchess turned toward Josiah, Selwyn leaped forward, grabbing the pendant and jerking it from her, breaking the golden chain in the process. With a shriek of rage, the evil woman vanished from the solar.

Selwyn hurled the pendant with all his might, shattering it against the stone wall of the solar.

"Where am I?" Gilda looked confused and frightened as she gazed around the solar. "Josiah, where are we? How did we get here?"

Josiah hugged her joyfully. "Praise His Majesty for his goodness, you are all right!" he exulted. "Selwyn, let's get her home."

"Josiah," Gilda asked, continuing to gaze around the dusty solar, "what are we doing here?"

"It's a long story, my love," Josiah replied. "Right now we need to get you out of this wretched castle. I'll tell you all about it as we ride home."

Chapter Nineteen

The Castle of Faith was a welcome sight as Princess Gilda, Prince Josiah, and Prince Selwyn rode over the crest of a hill and saw the gleaming walls in the distance, painted deep crimson by the setting sun. "I can't wait to get home," Gilda said softly, and Josiah felt a surge of gratitude within his heart.

Selwyn stood in the stirrups. "I'll race you both to the front gate," he challenged. "First one on the drawbridge wins. I'll even give you a ten-length head start."

Josiah laughed. "Right. Gilda and I are riding double, while your horse carries just you! What do you think are our chances of winning?"

"I'll give you a twenty-length head start."

Josiah shook his head. "This is a moment of joy as Gilda returns to the castle. I have petitioned His Majesty for this many times. Let's just ride in at leisure."

Selwyn nodded to show that he understood.

The Castle of Faith disappeared from view for several minutes as the trio rode through a wooded area. As they emerged from the woods on a little hill four or five furlongs northeast of the castle, Selwyn reined to a stop and cried out, "Josiah! Look!"

Josiah reined in beside him. "No!" he cried. "No! Selwyn, this is the day that we have feared!"

The Castle of Faith was surrounded by a vast army of dark warriors. The moors to the north, east, and south of the castle were filled with cursing warriors and angry peasants preparing to storm the walls. Several battleships flying Argamor's flag were anchored in the bay just below the castle. A number of catapults, trebuchets, and other machines of war perched less than two hundred paces from the moat, poised for a direct assault. A massive battering ram lay at the edge of the moat, ready for action. Atop the battlements of the castle, Emmanuel's archers unleashed a volley of arrows into the vast hordes of dark warriors, with little result.

"Quickly—into the woods, lest they see us!" Josiah urged. He wheeled his horse and rode back into the forest with Selwyn following closely. The trio dismounted, tied the horses, and then crept back to the edge of the tree line. Crouching in the bushes, they took in the disheartening scene below.

"There must be millions of dark warriors," Gilda cried in anguish.

"Tens of thousands, at the very least," Josiah replied. "I fear that the Castle of Faith is lost!"

"Look," Selwyn said. "There are many peasants among the dark knights, fighting together against the castle. Why would the peasants fight against us?"

"They are fighting against Emmanuel, not against us," Josiah replied softly.

As Emmanuel's three children watched, two tall siege towers slowly rolled across the battlefield toward the castle. Crews of dark warriors worked busily around the catapults and trebuchets as they prepared to fire the dreaded weapons. Gilda noticed several long lines of dark warriors slowly advancing toward the castle. One by one, each knight stepped to the edge of the moat and then turned away to make room for the next warrior. The princess turned to her husband. "Josiah, what are they doing?" she asked, pointing to the unusual activity.

Josiah's heart sank. "They're filling in the moat," he replied sadly. "Each warrior is carrying a large boulder and casting it into the moat. Once the moat is filled in, that will give them access to the outer castle curtain!"

"Filling in the moat?" Selwyn echoed. "Josiah, that's impossible! Do you know how long it would take to fill the moat with boulders? It would take forever!"

"Not with this many warriors," Josiah replied. "Once a small area of the moat is filled in, they can build a platform right to the edge of the outer curtain, roll their siege towers across it, and gain access to the battlements."

Gilda began to weep. "Is there nothing we can do?"

Josiah was already opening his book. "We need to send petitions to Emmanuel." Hurriedly, he wrote a desperate message:

> *"My Lord, King Emmanuel:*
> *The Castle of Faith is in desperate straits as countless thousands of evil warriors are preparing to storm the walls and take the castle. My Lord, what are we to do? Please, I implore you, protect the castle.*
>
> *Your son, Josiah."*

Raising his hand, he released the parchment and watched as it shot over the treetops on its way to the Golden City. Moments later, Gilda and Selwyn also sent petitions.

"How are we to get into the castle?" Selwyn wondered aloud. "There is no way to fight our way through that horde!"

"I see no way in," Josiah replied soberly. "No way at all."

Weeping, Princess Gilda threw her arms around her husband.

"I am so sorry," she sobbed. "But for me, you would both be safe within the castle."

"Let's not worry about that," he told her gently. "You have been forgiven. Right now, the Castle of Faith hardly seems like a safe haven, anyway."

"But it is our home."

Josiah nodded. "And it is where we belong. But for now, there simply is no way back in."

As he spoke, one of the catapults released, sending a huge boulder skyward. The trio cringed as they watched the deadly projectile soar over the castle walls to land within the west bailey with a resounding crash.

"Petitions!" Josiah urged. "We must continue to send petitions!"

Prince Josiah had just released a second petition and then cringed as he saw an enormous boulder shoot skyward from the center catapult. His chagrin turned to astonishment as he saw the deadly missile suddenly explode in midair and become a cloud of harmless dust. Moments later a trebuchet released a huge spear into the air. Dread seized Josiah's heart as he watched the deadly missile speed toward the castle. But the dreadful spear abruptly stopped in midair and fell into the ranks of dark warriors as if it had been deflected by a stone wall.

The princess and the princes continued to send desperate petitions to Emmanuel as they watched the vast hordes of dark knights and peasants assault their beloved castle. At last, darkness stole across the land and a crescent moon peeked over the hills to the east. Clouds swept across the skies and obscured the light of the moon. Across the moors, fires sprang up here and there as the evil troops made camp.

"I'm glad the night is finally here," Gilda observed. "The darkness will protect the castle from further assault."

"These evil warriors are creatures of darkness, rather than light," Josiah told her. "This is perhaps when they will do the most damage."

"Where will we spend the night?" Gilda worried. "I wish there was a way to get back into the castle."

"I have petitioned the King in that regard," Josiah told her, "but for now, I see no way in. It would be impossible to fight our way through those hordes."

"Prince Josiah," a low voice called, and Josiah and his companions jumped in fright. The young prince drew his sword as a dark figure crept furtively toward their hiding place. "Prince Josiah, come with me," the voice said, and a powerfully built knight approached. "I have been sent to guide you into the castle."

"There is another way inside?" Josiah was incredulous.

"Aye, my lord, but we have to hurry," came the terse reply. "There is not a moment to lose. We can only get in at low tide, and that is now. If we delay, the opportunity will be lost. Follow me. You'll have to leave your horses where they are."

"Who are you?" Josiah asked, studying the huge warrior and noticing that his armor seemed to glow.

"My name is Olympas, my lord."

"Are you from the Castle of Faith?"

"I am."

"How long have you been there? I do not recall seeing you there."

Olympas hesitated. "I was assigned there recently. Come—we must not delay." The huge warrior led them deeper into the woods. "We'll have to move quietly and walk carefully, for the enemy is everywhere. Please, my lords and my lady—do not speak. Simply follow me in silence."

Ten minutes later, Olympas led his three charges into the

waters of the Bay of Opportunity. Gilda drew back. "We—we're going into the sea?"

"The tide is out right now, my lady," Olympas whispered. "But we must make haste, for it will soon return. Follow me, for this is the only way into the castle."

Moving slowly and cautiously, the four waded into the waters and made their way through a maze of slick, dark rocks that jutted from the water. When they reached chest-deep water, Olympas lit a torch. "We must hurry," he said tersely, "lest the enemy see the light and come to investigate."

The huge warrior held the torch close to the water and his young charges could see a dark opening beneath the rocks. "This is a natural cavern that leads beneath the foundation of the castle," Olympas explained. "No one in the castle, not even Sir Faithful, knows of its existence. But we must hurry, for right now there is less than two feet of space between the water and the ceiling of the cavern. Once the cavern floods, the entrance will be sealed off until the next low tide."

He looked at Josiah. "You go first, my lord."

Josiah's heart pounded furiously as he ducked deeper into the water and scrambled into the darkness of the cavern. The water lapped at his chin. Selwyn followed, and then Gilda. "This way, my lords and my lady," Olympas said, as his torch brightened the grotto. He led the way to the far end of the cavern.

"This will be the most difficult part of the journey," he told them, "but it will also be the shortest. When I give the signal, I want you to take a deep breath and then plunge down into the opening that I will show you. You will have to crawl or swim underwater for a distance of ten or twelve yards and then you will emerge into an undersea cavern that is lit by another torch. We will go through one by one—simply wait beside the torch until all of us are together again."

He smiled at Josiah. "Well, my lord, it looks as if you are first again. My right foot is right now at the edge of the tunnel. Take a deep breath, find my foot underwater, and then make your way through the tunnel. It will seem like a long way, but it is only ten or twelve yards at most. Ready, my lord?"

Josiah's heart constricted with fear as he plunged beneath the water. Scrambling as fast as he could, he half crawled, half swam through the submerged tunnel. At last, gasping for breath, he emerged from the water in a dark, subterrestrian chamber lit by one sputtering torch. Moments later, Selwyn's head popped up from the water, and then Gilda's.

The three Royal Ones followed the huge warrior into a narrow, twisting corridor that wound its way down into the base of the promontory. After following the dark passageway for several minutes, Olympas led his three charges through a narrow doorway and out into a moonlit courtyard. "Why, this is the west bailey!" Selwyn exclaimed in astonishment. "We're in the west bailey!"

"This is incredible," Gilda breathed.

"How did you know about the tunnel?" Josiah asked, turning to Olympas. He stared in utter astonishment. The huge warrior was gone, as was the doorway in the wall. Both had vanished without a trace.

The morning sun was just beginning to cast its golden rays across Terrestria as Prince Josiah, Prince Selwyn, and Sir Faithful stood high in the battlements of the northwest tower, gravely surveying the disheartening battle scene below. As far as the eye could see, the moors and plains beyond the Castle of Faith were filled with raging dark warriors intent on taking the castle and all who lived within its walls. Just as Josiah had predicted, the enemy had been hard at work all through the night. Incredible as it seemed, the castle moat had been filled with boulders; planks had been laid across the stones; and hundreds of evil knights were slowly rolling the two tremendous siege towers into position against the outer curtain walls.

Planks had also been laid across the moat in front of the main gate, and a company of dark warriors were moving the huge battering ram into position for an attack on the drawbridge and the gate.

As they watched, Emmanuel's archers sent a constant barrage of arrows against the enemy troops in a desperate attempt to thwart the attack. But the effort seemed futile—as soon as one dark knight was hit, another leaped forward to take his place. Foot by foot, the towers rolled forward.

"When did they first attack?" Selwyn asked.

"Yesterday about mid-afternoon," Sir Faithful answered. "A delegation from the Village of Dedication came to the castle and ordered me to cease flying Emmanuel's standards above the castle; or at least, remove the cross from his coat of arms." He paused. "It seems that it is the cross that offends people."

Josiah snorted. "They ordered you to remove the cross? The Village of Dedication is protected by the Castle of Faith! You would think they would be grateful!"

"So it would seem," the steward agreed.

"And most of the villagers respect and revere Emmanuel's coat of arms," Selwyn added. "They are grateful that it flies above the castle."

Sir Faithful sighed. "Aye, but the delegation informed me that there are a few residents that take offense at the sight of the cross on Emmanuel's standards. I was to take down the standards so as to not offend them."

"And you refused," Josiah offered.

"Aye. The next thing we knew, Argamor's dark forces were marching against the castle." He glanced down at the vast hordes of dark warriors. "But the Castle of Faith is not the only one—Argamor is attacking every one of Emmanuel's castles in Terrestria!"

"It doesn't look good," Josiah lamented, with a heavy heart. "The Castle of Faith is doomed."

"This is Emmanuel's castle," the steward replied sharply. "Prince Josiah, how is it that you have served your King this many years and yet you still don't know his mighty power?"

Josiah was silent. His thoughts went back to the incredible battles he had seen while touring the Book of the Apocalypse. Emmanuel's power had superseded anything that he had imagined. It didn't seem possible, but perhaps there was hope for the castle.

"Josiah, stay here in the tower and continue to send petitions."

Sir Faithful turned to Selwyn. "Come with me. We must prepare for the enemy's assault on the main gate."

"What about Gilda?" Josiah asked.

"At present, she is carrying supplies to the archers on the walls. Should the enemy forces scale the walls or penetrate the gate, she and the other women of the castle will seek shelter in the corridor below the great hall." The steward turned away.

"Sir Faithful?"

The steward turned back. "Aye, my prince?"

"If I don't see you and Selwyn again—" Josiah's voice broke.

"The situation is desperate, my prince," Sir Faithful said softly, "but this is Emmanuel's castle. Trust in his great love for you, and in his infinite power."

Selwyn stepped close to Josiah. The two young princes

grasped hands for a brief moment. "I love you, my brother," Josiah said huskily.

"And I you," Selwyn replied, looking deeply into Josiah's eyes. "Send petitions for me, will you?"

Unable to speak, Josiah simply nodded. As Selwyn and Sir Faithful hurried down the tower stairs, Josiah knelt and began to write an urgent petition.

The battle for the Castle of Faith seemed hopeless. Although Emmanuel's knights atop the battlements fought valiantly to prevent it, the dark warriors were able to move the siege towers within a few feet of the outer curtain walls. At the same time, the company of dark knights manning the enormous battering ram had vigorously assaulted the drawbridge and main gate, with telling effects. Just as the siege towers dropped their ramps atop the walls, discharging scores of dark knights screaming with rage, the main gate splintered and gave way with a crash that resounded throughout the castle. Dark knights by the hundreds flooded through the gate. Thus, the outer curtain wall had been breached at three points simultaneously. The enemy was now within the castle.

"Retreat!" The command came from the lips of Captain Watchful, and to Josiah it sounded the death knell of the Castle of Faith. Rolling yet another petition tightly, he glanced down into the barbican as he released the parchment. The castle constable and an entire garrison of knights were battling for their lives, fighting desperately to hold the mob of dark warriors and peasants at bay as the defenders attempted to retreat to the safety of the inner wall.

Josiah had mere seconds to make a decision. If he fled the

tower now, he could make it to the battlements of the inner curtain wall just ahead of the hordes of dark knights. In their last stand for the castle, perhaps he could be reunited with Gilda. If he stayed where he was he would be safe for a time, for the trapdoor at his feet was eight inches thick and could be secured with six heavy bolts. Once he secured the trapdoor, the only way an enemy knight could gain access to his position would be to scale the outside of the tower, and he knew that no one would attempt that. Burning him out would take hours. He would be safe for the moment.

Should I stay in the tower and continue to send petitions as Sir Faithful requested, or should I try to reach Gilda? It seemed that his heart was being torn in two. Tears streamed down his face as he knelt and began securing the heavy bolts at his feet.

Chapter Twenty

High in the northwest tower of the Castle of Faith, Josiah watched with a heavy heart as the battle unfolded below him. The castle was being destroyed by the angry hordes of dark knights and Terrestrian peasants, and the castle residents were fighting for their lives. As Josiah watched, continuing to send petitions, the evil forces of dark knights attacked the inner gate with a vengeance, screaming their hatred for Emmanuel as they slammed the battering ram against the gate again and again. In spite of the young prince's fervent petitions, the enemy warriors and their peasant counterparts seemed to be winning the battle for the Castle of Faith.

A company of dedicated archers atop the battlements did their best to hold the enemy at bay as they sent a constant barrage of arrows into the screaming, cursing ranks. Other warriors poured boiling water down to impede the assault with the deadly battering ram. But all to no avail.

Where is Gilda? Is she all right? Oh, that I could be with her! For one brief moment, Josiah regretted his decision to stay in the tower. Tears streamed down his face as he knelt to write yet another desperate petition.

> "My Lord, King Emmanuel:
> Hear me, my King, I beg you. Your faithfulness is great and you
> have never failed me, yet the Castle of Faith is being destroyed,
> my Lord, and your children are fighting for their lives. The
> situation is desperate and we are in extreme peril. My Lord,
> save us.
>
> > Your son, Josiah."

The petition soared from his hand seconds later, but Josiah did not even watch it go. *Why does King Emmanuel not answer? Does he no longer care? Are we to be destroyed by these vile warriors who now curse Emmanuel's name within his own castle?*

Shouts of victory drew Josiah's attention down to the bailey and in horror he realized that the swarms of dark knights had managed to open the inner gates and gain access to the bailey. His heart sank as he watched the cursing hordes of evil warriors and peasants flood into the courtyard. The castle residents fled in terror.

A trumpet sounded just then, loud and clear and strong, and the golden notes resounded triumphantly across the skies, echoing and re-echoing across the moors until it seemed that all of Terrestria rang with the sound. At that moment, Josiah's feet left the battlements of the tower and he found himself soaring upwards through the Terrestrian skies above the Castle of Faith.

"The King has returned!" he cried joyfully, as he realized what was happening. "I shall see his face! King Emmanuel has come back for me! This is the moment I have been longing for!"

At that moment he realized that he was surrounded by multitudes of Emmanuel's children. He stared in amazement. None wore armor; all were dressed in shimmering white robes so dazzling that it almost hurt the eyes to look at them. His own armor was gone; in its place was a shimmering white robe.

"Josiah!"

He turned at the sound of his name to find his lovely wife at his elbow, dressed in white and looking lovelier than he had ever seen her. He reached for her.

"Welcome, my dear children, welcome!" cried a majestic voice that rang across the heavens. Josiah turned to see King Emmanuel standing upon a cloud with his arms outstretched in loving welcome. His white robe and golden crown glistened with a brilliance that rivaled the sun. "My children, come with me to your new home!"

Josiah gazed with awe upon the loving face of his King. "My Lord, Emmanuel," he whispered. "My King, I will love you forever."

In the twinkling of an eye, the vast throng of white-robed Royal Ones found themselves descending toward the majestic golden gates of the Golden City of the Redeemed. Cries of victory and praise went up at the sight of the magnificent city. As their feet touched the banks of the beautiful river, a fanfare of majestic trumpets sounded in welcome, loud and clear and strong. The skies above the city rang with the sound.

Josiah glanced at Gilda and saw a radiance upon her face like the glow of the rising sun. She smiled. "We're home, Josiah! Finally home!"

A host of shining ones stood in the enormous gate of the city, personally welcoming each of Emmanuel's children to their new home. Songs of praise and adoration for Emmanuel filled the air. The atmosphere in the Golden City was that of eager anticipation.

Overwhelming joy flooded Josiah's soul as he walked through the golden gate and entered the Golden City of the Redeemed. *Unworthy*, he thought. *I am so unworthy to be here.*

"Papa!"

Josiah turned to see a small, white-robed figure dashing toward him. "Ethan!"

With cries of joy, the little boy leaped into his father's arms. "Welcome home, Papa! I couldn't wait till you got here! There is so much that I want to show you!"

Tears of joy flowed as Josiah hugged his son. "Oh, Ethan, Ethan! My Little Knight!"

Ethan pulled away and looked strangely at him. "There are no knights in the Golden City, Papa, for there is no enemy here. I could not be King Emmanuel's knight, but I am his servant." Josiah's heart thrilled at the words of his son.

Suddenly the little boy wriggled down and ran down the golden street with cries of joy. "Mama!" He leaped into Gilda's arms and the tears of joy flowed again.

A vast throng of millions of white-robed royalty lined both sides of the golden street. Songs of praise to King Emmanuel filled the air. All eyes turned toward the magnificent gate as his grateful children waited breathlessly.

Ethan tugged at Josiah's hand. "Do you know what is going to happen, Papa? This is the moment that all of Terrestria and all of Eternity have been waiting for! This is King Emmanuel's coronation day! Today we will crown Emmanuel as King of kings and Lord of lords, and then we will live with him and praise him forever!"

Gratitude welled up within Josiah's soul. "I know, Ethan, and this is going to be one glorious day."

"Papa, will we ever go back to the Castle of Faith? Will we ever go back to Terrestria?"

"Aye, son, we will. We'll go back to Terrestria for a thousand years and it will be marvelous, for King Emmanuel will reign among us."

Selwyn moved close to Josiah. "The Golden City is more

than just a city," he whispered in awe. "It's a country!"

Josiah gazed in wonder. As far as the eye could see, the glittering city lay before them, enchanting in its beauty and splendor. Enormous mansions of glistening white marble. Golden boulevards whose lustrous surface reflected the majestic mountains in the distance. Spacious lawns shaded by luscious fruit trees of all varieties. Brilliant wildflowers of spectacular beauty, their gentle fragrance filling the air. A crystal stream flowing like a living diamond. Songbirds filling the air with their music while hummingbirds darted from flower to flower, rare jewels of color and beauty. And high above the city, a brilliant rainbow with seven dazzling colors.

"Such incredible beauty," Selwyn said softly. "Such grandeur. It's as if our eyes can't take it all in."

"And best of all," Josiah replied joyfully, "we'll be with our King forever."

Trumpets sounded a majestic fanfare, and the city suddenly blazed with brilliant white light. Dazzling beams of color flashed across the skies like multi-colored bolts of lightning. The air was charged with anticipation. Josiah turned.

King Emmanuel had stepped through the magnificent golden gate. His glory filled the city, radiating from the skies, reflecting from polished marble walls, glistening in the golden streets, illuminating each face with a glorious radiance. Thousands upon thousands of shining ones descended from the rainbow in the skies to hover on shimmering wings, radiating fiery flashes of color and light as their song of praise rang across the countryside.

A moment of sheer joy swept over Josiah's soul as he realized that the grandest coronation of the ages was about to commence.

"All hail His Majesty, King Emmanuel!" a mighty voice cried from the skies. "Emmanuel, King of kings and Lord of lords!"

Josiah and the millions of white-robed Redeemed Ones dropped to their faces in reverence and adoration. The shining ones folded their wings, bowed their heads, and floated gently downward to kneel in reverence before the Kings of kings. Silence reigned in the Golden City of the Redeemed.

King Emmanuel walked slowly, majestically down the golden street, his countenance radiating love and welcome as he made eye contact with each and every one of his trembling sons and daughters.

Emmanuel's loving gaze fell upon Josiah and the young prince was overwhelmed to find himself face to face with the Lord of Eternity. Gazing wonderingly into the knowing, loving eyes of King Emmanuel, Josiah suddenly found a deep, settled peace. A gentle love radiated from the King, and he felt secure in its warmth. "My King," he said softly, "I will love you and serve you forever!"

The End Times

The wicked and righteous are at war.
A war that's eternally old;
The wicked are bound to Argamor,
Doomed to fail, but blindly bold.

Yet they despise the righteous few,
And defame Emmanuel's Name:
They e'er assail the right and true,
Without a trace of shame.

The righteous remnant of the King
Their happy, hopeful praises tell.
They work, they fight, they pray, they sing,
To mighty King Emmanuel.

They are a group, a pilgrim band,
Though often scorned to face.
They're going to a better land,
And petition for His grace.

They follow on the narrow way,
And gladly wait their King's return.
Aye, eagerly they watch and pray –
Expectantly they yearn.

He will return as lightning flash,
Quick as the twinkling of an eye.
The trump shall sound as thunder crash,
As the righteous rise on high.

They shall meet Him in the skies,
Forever His grace and mercy tell.
In golden courts receive the prize
From loving King Emmanuel.

by Zachary O. Cox

Glossary

Bailey: the courtyard in a castle.

Barbican: the space or courtyard between the inner and outer walls of a castle.

Battlement: on castle walls, a parapet with openings behind which archers would shelter when defending the castle.

Castle: a fortified building or complex of buildings, used both for defense and as the residence for the lord of the surrounding land.

Catapult: a large war machine with a long tension arm capable of hurling boulders or other projectiles great distances.

Coat of arms: an arrangement of heraldic emblems, usually depicted on a shield or standard, indicating ancestry and position.

Couter: the part of the armor that protected a knight's elbow.

Curtain: the protective wall of a castle.

Daub-and-wattle: construction technique in which a mixture of clay or mud is applied over a mat woven of sticks and reeds.

Doublet: a close-fitting garment worn by men.

Furlong: a measurement of distance equal to one-eighth of a mile.

Garrison: a group of soldiers stationed in a castle.

Gatehouse: a fortified structure built over the gateway to a castle.

Gauntlet: armor for the knight's hand, usually lined with leather.

Great hall: the room in a castle where the meals were served and the main events of the day occurred.

Greave: plate armor protecting a knight's lower leg, usually consisting of front and back pieces.

Lute: a stringed musical instrument having a long, fretted neck and a hollow, pear-shaped body.

Minstrel: a traveling entertainer who sang and recited poetry.

Moat: a deep, wide ditch surrounding a castle, often filled with water.

Murder holes: large holes in the floor of the castle gatehouse, through which castle defenders would drop large boulders on attacking warriors.

Portcullis: a heavy wooden grating covered with iron and suspended on chains above the gateway or any doorway of a castle. The portcullis could be lowered quickly to seal off an entrance if the castle was attacked.

Siege tower: a movable tower used in an assault on a castle. When the tower was placed close to a castle wall, attacking knights could climb stairs inside and exit the tower at the top of the castle wall, thus gaining entrance to the castle.

Sentry walk: a platform or walkway around the inside top of a castle curtain used by guards, lookouts and archers defending a castle.

Solar: a private sitting room or bedroom designated for royalty or nobility.

Standard: a long, tapering flag or ensign, as of a king or a nation.

Stone: a British unit of weight equal to fourteen pounds.

Trebuchet: a large war machine with a pivoted arm having a large weight at one end and a sling for missiles at the other.

Tunic: a loose-fitting, long-sleeved garment.

Vambrace: the part of a knight's plate armor which protected his arm.

Knights and Castles

- Early knights wore body armor made of chain mail – small, linked metal rings.

- Weapons such as war hammers and two-handed swords could pass through chain mail quite easily.

- Over the years, steel plates were added to give knights more protection.

- Under his armor, a knight wore a padded arming doublet.

- The doublet had waxed leather thongs for lacing through holes in the plate armor.

- A knight always dressed from the feet up – sabotons protecting the feet went on first.

- Greaves protected the knight's lower legs; poleyns protected his knees; cuisses protected his thighs.

- The breastplate and backplate together were called the cuirass. They were fastened together at the shoulders and held together at the waist by leather straps.

- Tassets, which protected the abdomen and upper thighs, were attached to the breastplate.

- The knight's arms were protected by vambraces; his elbows, by couters; his hands, by gauntlets lined with leather.

- The knight's helmet was lined for comfort and to protect his head from heavy blows.

- Knights needed help from their squires in dressing for battle.

Preparing for the King's Return

Just as King Emmanuel returned to Terrestria to take his children to the Golden City, our King, the Lord Jesus Christ, will one day return to take his children to heaven. We believe that it will happen very soon—we need to be ready! Here's how to prepare for the King's return:

Admit that you are a sinner. The Bible tells us: *"For all have sinned, and come short of the glory of God."* (Romans 3:23) We have done wrong things and sinned against God. Our sin will keep us from heaven and condemn us to hell. We need to be forgiven.

Believe that Jesus died for you. The Bible says: *"But God commendeth his love toward us, in that, while we were yet sinners, Christ died for us."* (Romans 5:8) The King of kings, the Lord Jesus Christ, became a man and died for our sins on the cross, shedding his blood for us so that we can be forgiven. Three days later, he arose from the grave.

Call on Jesus to save you. The Bible says: *"For whosoever shall call upon the name of the Lord shall be saved."* (Romans 10:13) Admit to God that you are a sinner. Believe that Jesus died for you on the cross and then came back to life in three days. Call on Jesus in faith and ask him to save you. He will! And when he saves you from your sin, he adopts you into his royal family. Once you become a child of the King, you can know that when he returns he will take you to heaven to be with him.

You should also know that those who reject King Jesus will be left here on earth when he returns. These people will go through the terrible judgments briefly described in this book. Worst of all, they will not see heaven, but instead, will be lost forever.

Preparing for the King's Return

Just as King Emmanuel returned to Terrestria to take his children to the Golden City, our King, the Lord Jesus Christ, will one day return to take his children to heaven. We believe that it will happen very soon—we need to be ready! Here's how to prepare for the King's return:

Admit that you are a sinner. The Bible tells us: *"For all have sinned, and come short of the glory of God." (Romans 3:23)* We have done wrong things and sinned against God. Our sin will keep us from heaven and condemn us to hell. We need to be forgiven.

Believe that Jesus died for you. The Bible says: *"But God commendeth his love toward us, in that, while we were yet sinners, Christ died for us." (Romans 5:8)* The King of kings, the Lord Jesus Christ, became a man and died for our sins on the cross, shedding his blood for us so that we can be forgiven. Three days later, he arose from the grave.

Call on Jesus to save you. The Bible says: *"For whosoever shall call upon the name of the Lord shall be saved." (Romans 10:13)* Admit to God that you are a sinner. Believe that Jesus died for you on the cross and then came back to life in three days. Call on Jesus in faith and ask him to save you. He will! And when he saves you from your sin, he adopts you into his royal family. Once you become a child of the King, you can know that when he returns he will take you to heaven to be with him.

You should also know that those who reject King Jesus will be left here on earth when he returns. These people will go through the terrible judgments briefly described in this book. Worst of all, they will not see heaven, but instead, will be lost forever.

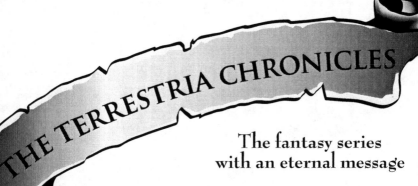